Viking

Frontispiece: Grace and her father William Darling rowing out to rescue the shipwrecked crew of the *Forfarshire* steamer – *c.*1845, anon

GRACE HAD AN ENGLISH HEART

Jessica Mitford

VIKING

VIKING

Published by the Penguin Group
27 Wrights Lane, London W8 5TZ, England
Viking Penguin Inc., 40 West 23rd Street, New York, New York 10010, USA
Penguin Books Australia Ltd, Ringwood, Victoria, Australia
Penguin Books Canada Ltd, 2801 John Street, Markham, Ontario, Canada L3R 1B4
Penguin Books (NZ) Ltd, 182–190 Wairau Road, Auckland 10, New Zealand

Penguin Books Ltd, Registered Offices: Harmondsworth, Middlesex, England

First published 1988

Filmset in 11/13 pt Trump by Wyvern Typesetting Ltd, Bristol

Printed in Great Britain by
Butler and Tanner Ltd, Frome and London
Designed by Tessa Pellow

British Library Cataloguing in Publication Data

Mitford, Jessica
   Grace had an English heart.
   1. Darling, Grace, *1815–1842*
   2. Heroines —— English —— Biography
   I. Title
   942.07′092′4   DA565.D2

ISBN 0–670–81202–1

To
my niece
EMMA TENNANT

Previous books by Jessica Mitford

Hons and Rebels 1960
The American Way of Death 1963
The Trial of Dr Spock 1969
The American Prison Business 1973
A Fine Old Conflict 1977
The Making of a Muckraker 1979
Faces of Philip: a Portrait of Philip Toynbee 1984

CONTENTS

'All boatmen are Grace Darlings to me.'

Anthony Blanche, at Oxford Eights Week,
in *Brideshead Revisited*, 1945

Before me, upon the desk where I am writing, lies a lock of soft brown hair, which, as a stray sunbeam glances upon it, becomes tinged with ruddy gold.

This little curl, fine as spun silk, is my one relic of the heroine Grace Darling, who, fifty years ago this very autumn, was laid to rest in the old churchyard of Bamborough, Northumberland, four years after the deed of daring which made the whole country ring with her praise.

Florence Balgarnie, in
The Young Woman, 1892

GRACE DARLING One of the first Hybrid Teas to achieve popularity. Shapely, creamy white flowers shaded with pink. Moderately vigorous. 1884.

Peter Beales's Rose Catalogue, 1986

List of Colour Plates

Two portraits of Grace Darling by H. P. Parker, 1838 (*Eddie Ryle-Hodges*)

Portrait of Grace's father by H. P. Parker, 1838 (*Eddie Ryle-Hodges*)

Portrait of Grace's mother by H. P. Parker, 1838 (*Eddie Ryle-Hodges*)

Bonnet donated to Grace (*Eddie Ryle-Hodges*)

Items of Grace's clothing (*Eddie Ryle-Hodges*)

View of Bamburgh by T. Sutherland, after T. M. Richardson, 1820 (*Victoria and Albert Museum*)

'Wreck of the *Forfarshire* steamer', by Leitch, from a drawing by J. W. Carmichael (*Eddie Ryle-Hodges*)

Portrayal of the rescue by William Bell Scott (*Victoria and Albert Museum*)

The Farne Islands today in more clement conditions (*Aerofilms Ltd*)

Pottery inspired by Grace Darling (*Eddie Ryle-Hodges*)

Offer for a Grace Darling statuette on a Captain Morgan rum bottle (*Eddie Ryle-Hodges*)

'Royal Doulton salutes Grace Darling', 1987 (*Eddie Ryle-Hodges*)

Grace Darling window at Bamburgh church (*Eddie Ryle-Hodges*)

Photograph of Grace Darling's tomb, reconstructed in 1885 (*Eddie Ryle-Hodges*)

List of Black and White Illustrations

The Grace Darling Song

'Twas on the Longstone lighthouse,
  There dwelt an English maid:
Pure as the air around her,
  Of danger ne'er afraid.
One morning just at daybreak,
  A storm toss'd wreck she spied;
And tho' to try seemed madness,
  'I'll save the crew!' she cried.

CHORUS
  And she pull'd away, o'er the rolling seas,
    Over the waters blue.
  'Help! Help!' she could hear the cry of the
                          shipwreck'd crew.
  But Grace had an English heart,
    And the raging storm she brav'd;
  She pull'd away, mid the dashing spray,
    And the crew she saved.

They to the rock were clinging,
  A crew of nine all told;
Between them and the lighthouse,
  The sea like mountains rolled.
Said Grace: 'Come help me, Father,
  We'll launch that boat,' said she.
Her father cried: ' 'Tis madness,
  To face that raging sea!'

                          CHORUS

One murmur'd prayer 'Heav'n guard us!'
  And then they were afloat;
Between them and destruction,
  The planks of that frail boat.
Then spoke the maiden's father:
  'Return or doom'd are we.'
But up spoke brave Grace Darling:
  'Alone I'll brave the sea!'

                          CHORUS

They bravely rode the billows,
  And reached the rock at length:
They saved the storm toss'd sailors,
  In Heaven alone their strength.
Go, tell the wide world over,
  What English pluck can do;
And sing of brave Grace Darling,
  Who nobly saved the crew.

                          CHORUS

Music of the Grace Darling Song

'Twas on the Long-stone light-house, There dwelt an Eng - lish maid; Pure as the air a -
- round her, Of dan - ger ne'er a - fraid; One morn - ing just at day - break, A
storm-toss'd wreck she spied; And tho' to try seemed mad - ness, 'I'll save the crew!' she cried.

Chorus
Tempo di Valse

And she pull'd a - way, o'er the rol - ling sea, O - ver the wa - ters blue. _____
'Help! Help!' she could hear the cry of the ship - wreck'd crew. _____ But
Grace had an Eng - lish heart, _____ And the ra - ging storm she brav'd _____ She
pull'd a - way, mid the dash - ing spray, And the crew she saved. _____

1. GRACE HAD AN ENGLISH HEART

Who was Grace Darling? Her name is virtually unknown in America, but to this day is recognized, albeit dimly, throughout Britain; she has become to a younger generation a semi-folkloric character, akin, say, to Queen Boadicea or Lady Godiva, whose existence had some basis in historical fact but whose legend had far outstripped reality.

For the British of both sexes and all ages the name seems to stir a sort of faint tribal memory, although full of error as to details. For most women over the age of forty it evokes the image of a young Victorian beauty, her long hair flowing behind her as she rows all alone through mountainous waves towards a shipwreck dimly discerned in the background; this is the picture they remember from those ghastly illustrated girls' annuals inflicted each Christmas by kindly aunts.

The annuals were a *mélange* of uplifting short stories, instruction in the household arts of cooking and sewing, and inspirational messages, intended to foster in the young reader attributes and habits of mind deemed appropriate to her sex: industriousness, obedience, modesty, piety. Grace Darling was a perfect exemplar of these virtues.

(There were also the boys' annuals, throbbing with adventure stories, the lives of intrepid explorers and war heroes, great inventions, scientific experiments, exhorting the reader to the male virtues of courage, sportsmanship, kindness to animals – meaning dogs and horses, *not* foxes, partridges and pheasants. But these need not concern us here.)

My own introduction to Grace Darling was somewhat different. I do not remember being given the girls' annuals. Perhaps the Mitford aunts feared that the moral message contained therein would be lost on their wayward little nieces. But from earliest childhood I knew the story of the heroine and her noble deed from the stirring song (reproduced on pp. 16–17) that my sisters and I used to sing gathered round my mother's piano. From this, I learned that Grace had an English heart; was pure as the air around her, of danger ne'er afraid; and that her wretched father was an unmitigated coward, a laggard who cried ''Tis madness, to face that raging sea!' and then, just as they got afloat, 'Return or doom'd are we!' How awful of him, we all thought as we roared out the 'Help! Help!' of the shipwreck'd crew. (The song persisted unto the third generation. According to my sister Deborah, when my mother's many grandchildren were assembled to sing it at Inch Kenneth, her remote Hebridean island, the 'Help! Help!'s sometimes got so loud that boats would put out from neighbouring islands to see what was the matter.)

Years drifted by, and I gave no more thought to Grace Darling until one day, *circa* 1958, I was having lunch with an old friend, Lou Gottlieb, the talented leader of the Limelighters, a popular folksinging group then in much demand in American nightclubs, on college campuses, and for children's programmes. In the course of lunch, I first hummed, then whistled, then at Lou's insistence sang the Grace Darling Song – rather to the consternation of the restaurant's management who hovered anxiously during the 'Help! Help!'s. Instantly enthralled, Lou scribbled the words and melody on the back of the menu, vowing to include it in the Limelighters' repertoire.

There were a few hitches. Lou rang up to say that he had decided to change the words to 'Grace had a *Jewish* heart.' I was appalled – how unfair! surely, I pointed out, there are plenty of Jewish, Irish, black heroines – spare us our first authentic English heroine. He yielded on this, but did amend the chorus slightly, adding two more 'Help! Help!'s, to assure, as he explained, maximum audience participation. His additional lines ran: 'Grace had an English heart / And she knew how to handle an oar / Help! help! came the desperate yelp of the crew offshore.'

The song was first introduced by the Limelighters to an audience of Berkeley schoolchildren. Copy for the programme notes had been telephoned in, to the confusion of the printer who transcribed the title as 'Grey Starling'. The RCA Victor record of this event, entitled 'The

Limelighters: Through Children's Eyes', is now a collector's item. In fact the only exceptions to the aforementioned American ignorami on the subject are a few who still remember Lou's introduction to Grace: 'She was the daughter of a chicken-hearted lighthouse keeper!' they will exclaim, for such was Lou's unkind (and, as it turns out inaccurate) description of Mr Darling.

Shortly after the Limelighters' record appeared I was staying with my mother at Inch Kenneth. Poring over the *Daily Telegraph* (the only newspaper my mother took in, hence the sole source of daily intellectual nourishment) I spotted a tiny news item buried in an inside page, reporting litigation between Commander Phipps Hornby, Hon. Curator of the Grace Darling Museum and a pub, The Black Swan, over title to a relic of the wrecked ship *Forfarshire* whose crew Grace had rescued. The Grace Darling *Museum?* We had never heard of its existence. At my mother's direction, I wrote straight off to the Hon. Curator explaining our interest in this matter and informing him that my mother intended to bequeath the bound sheet music of the song to the museum.

I soon had his answer, written in exactly the style one might have expected from the pen of a personage whose letterhead, that of the Royal National Lifeboat Institution, announced him as Commander W. M. Phipps Hornby, RN, Honorary Curator, Grace Darling Museum, Bamburgh,* Northumberland.

17 August 1962
... I am afraid that the report that you read in the *Daily Telegraph* is not wholly accurate. (At the risk of appearing cynical: my impression is that newspaper reports rarely are!) What happened was that shortly after the luckless *Forfarshire* struck on the Big Harcar rock, in the Farnes, she broke in half. The stern portion sank at once; the forepart remained wedged on the rock and in due course was sold by auction. The forepart produced numerous relics, some of which we now have in the Grace Darling Museum. Others, including the nameplate to which I shall come in a moment, are to be found in private hands or perhaps in other museums.

---

*Spellings of place names vary in early accounts: Bamborough, Balmboro; Farnes Islands, Fern Islands; Big Harcar or Harker, etc. Except where quoting, I have used the current spelling.

He continues with a description of various *Forfarshire* relics, some authenticated, others not. As to the one in question:

The nameplate to which the *Daily Telegraph* article referred was in fact quite a large board, with 'Forfarshire' on it in gilt letters, that was discovered in the cellar of the Black Swan public house in Seahouses, under several layers of whitewash, in the course of redecoration. I hazarded the opinion that it might have come from the part of the wreck that remained on the Big Harcar.

A little later the landlord of the Black Swan retired, and sold the name board to a friend who was landlord of another 'pub' in Seahouses. The Brewers who owned the Black Swan then stepped in and claimed that the board was their property. And so the row started. Eventually, in a reserved judgement that followed upon an all-day hearing, the local County Court Judge pronounced in favour of the Brewers. So now the board once more adorns the bar parlour of the Black Swan; and incidentally constitutes a cause of covetousness to the Hon. Curator of the Grace Darling Museum. . .

The nameplate salvaged from the *Forfarshire* steamer in the Black Swan, Seahouses, with David Shiel (pointing), coxswain of the lifeboat at Seahouses, and Sheila and Billy Gilholm, landlord of the Black Swan

I had the letter photocopied and sent it to Lou Gottlieb. His reply:

21 October 1962

Dear Decca,

Commander Phipps Hornby n'existe pas! 'The luckless Forfarshire', 'the Big Harcar rock in the Farnes', the landlord of the Black Swan – the Royal National Life-boat Institution, in fact, the Grace Darling Museum itself are all ingredients for some kind of neo-Dickensian stew that you are cooking up which will no doubt assume epistolary form.

Beautiful, beautiful Britannia!

Vaya Cohen Deeose!

Lou

In the event, the 'Dickensian stew' stayed on the back burner for more than two decades, only to come a-simmer in 1985 as a result of a conversation with Tony Lacey of Viking/Penguin and Emma Tennant, the novelist, who were preparing a series of short biographical sketches under the general title 'Lives of Modern Women'. Several of these had already appeared: mini-biographies of Jean Rhys, Rebecca West, Freya Stark. Would I be interested in writing one for the series about, for example, Mrs Roosevelt? Well – no, said I. She has been the subject of several huge tomes, she figures prominently in all the memoirs of the day ... I don't think another is needed. How about Jackie Onassis? Double no – same reason. Those famous First Ladies tend to be overdone. What's left to say about them, except to crib from other people's work?

Then my husband, Bob Treuhaft, had an idea. How about Grace Darling? A flash of recognition – Tony and Emma were immediately enthusiastic, although as they pointed out, Grace, born 1815, died 1842, would hardly qualify as 'modern' for their series. And, they asked, what did I really know about Grace Darling except for that stirring ballad? For, at the mention of her name, I had burst into song, as though triggered by a Pavlovian reflex.

I did know a bit more, as kind friends and relations, having been subjected on late evenings to compulsory participation in singing the Grace Darling Song, had over the years sent me long-out-of-print books, among them *Grace Darling: Heroine of the Farne Islands. Her Life, and its Lessons. By the Author of 'Our Queen'*, published *circa* 1875 – thirty-three years after the death of the lighthouse heroine.

Aside from her incomparable prose style (for samples of which see chapter 9), the author of *Our Queen* recreates for the reader the pleasures and pains of being a subject of public adulation in 1838, one year after Victoria's accession to the throne. For example, soon after The Deed (as it is still reverently called in Northumberland) became known through newspaper accounts, twelve artists made the perilous journey o'er the rolling sea to do Grace's portrait. There were so many requests for locks of her hair that she was in danger of going bald. Suitors sought her hand in marriage; she withstood them all, and remained a modest, single maiden until her early death of consumption four years after the rescue.

She seems to have been the right girl in the right place at the right time to usher in the Victorian era. What could be a more appropriate ornament to the beginning of the eighteen-year-old Queen's reign than 'an English maid, pure as the air around her, of danger ne'er afraid'? She exemplified those virtues considered appropriate to a person of her age, sex and lowly station in life: chastity, humility, obedience to her parents, devotion to domestic tasks, piety ... As that quintessential Victorian bore, Charles Kingsley put it,

> Be good, sweet maid, and let who will be clever.

One can see why the English public were receptive to a heroine with these qualities. For many years they had endured the unpalatable reign of the dissolute and profligate Regent, and Victoria's ghastly uncles who shed their faithful old mistresses in order to marry within their rank, hoping to produce male children who would take precedence over their niece as heirs to the throne. 'I *will* be good,' said little Princess Victoria to her governess; and doubtless to the relief of many (although not all) of her subjects, goodness became the order of the day. Solid, unremitting virtue was the hallmark of her reign.

The Lighthouse Heroine fitted perfectly into this format – her very name seemed so extraordinarily apt, almost uncannily predictive of the special place she was destined to occupy in the warm and sentimental hearts of the early Victorians. As a contemporary newspaper noted,

It is not often that heroines of real life possess the advantageous attractions of a pretty name or a charming person; but Grace Darling has both. She would unquestionably have been loved and admired as heartily had she been Dorothy Dobbs, with a wide mouth, snub nose, and a squint; but it is pleasant to find coupled with a fine and generous nature a lovely face and a name at once euphonious and cherishable. Grace Darling! – poet or novelist need not desire one better fitted to bestow on a paragon of womanhood; we would fain see it embalmed in a sonnet by WORDSWORTH or a lyric by CAMPBELL; but it will 'live in her land's language', if not immortalized in verse.*

Yet puzzling, to me, was the circumstance of her instant fame and the durability of her legend over a span of almost a century and a half. I had supposed that newspaper-created 'personalities' were a twentieth-century product, originating in the perfervid headlines of the Yellow Press, such as the *Daily Mail*, *Express*, *Mirror* in England, and the Hearst newspapers in America. Later in this century, with the advent of *Time*, *Newsweek*, television and the assistance of public-relations firms, the manufacture of media celebrities has become routine. The example of *People* magazine is now slavishly followed by metropolitan newspapers in America and England with their sections called 'People in the News', 'Celebrity Watch', etc. All, one might have thought, a relatively modern development.

In fact, Grace Darling in her day was as celebrated by the press, as worshipped by her fans, as, say, the Beatles in our era. Her name lives on throughout the British Commonwealth. In September 1988, the 150th anniversary of the Deed, there will be a huge celebration in her honour at the museum in Bamburgh, to which people are expected to flock from as far away as Australia.

The museum has been gearing up for this event for the past few years. As the present Hon. Curator, Mr Derek Calderwood, confided in a conspiratorial whisper when I met him in 1985, 'It is almost certain that a member of the Royal Family will attend. But as you know, the Palace are very publicity-shy, so the less said the better.'

---

*Sunderland and Durham *County Herald*, 23 November 1838, quoting from the *Spectator*.

The publicity-shyness of the Palace may be questionable; but Grace Darling's shyness, her intense dislike of the public spotlight in which she suddenly and unexpectedly found herself, her resistance to the consequences of fame are well documented, through her own letters and a booklet, *Grace Darling: Her True Story*, published in 1880 by her sister Thomasin. In short, in contrast to the self-promoting celebrities of today, Grace not only did nothing to advance her fame and acclaim, she positively shrank from it.

Why, and how, did the Grace Darling legend originate, and what accounts for its remarkable persistence and longevity?

Portrait of the young Queen Victoria, 1843, by F. X. Winterhalter, lent by gracious permission of Her Majesty The Queen

In search of answers, I accumulated a large file of contemporary newspaper accounts of the wreck and rescue; a stack of girls' magazines spanning a century, from the 1850s to the 1950s; several biographies of Grace Darling, the earliest published in 1875, and the latest, a play performed throughout northern England in 1984.

I visited the Grace Darling Museum in Bamburgh with my niece Emma Tennant (not to be confused with the novelist of the same name), who lives not far from Darling territory. Later, she and I pulled away 'mid the dashing spray (or, more accurately, bought tickets for the trip in a commercial tour boat packed with sightseers) to the Longstone Lighthouse and environs, including a detour from the Longstone to the Big Harcar rock along the very route taken by Grace and her father in response to the cry of the shipwreck'd crew.

These, then, are the principal ingredients for the ensuing stew – not as spicy, perhaps, as might suit the jaded taste of modern palates, accustomed to the racy doings of filmstars and the younger members of the Royal Family, yet full of wholesome meat and potatoes of an earlier, more innocent age.

2. MELANCHOLY

As preamble, a bare-bones summary of the facts: The *Forfarshire*, one of the first of the luxury steamers, with approximately sixty crew and passengers on board, plus valuable cargo, was wrecked in a violent storm on Big Harcar Rock in the Farne Islands off the coast of Northumberland during the night of 6–7 September 1838. Eight crew members and a male passenger escaped in the ship's lifeboat. They were subsequently picked up by a passing sloop and deposited in nearby North Shields on the same evening.

At about 7 a.m. on 7 September, when it grew light enough to see, William Darling, keeper of the Longstone Lighthouse, and his twenty-two-year-old daughter Grace, descried the movement of people on Big Harcar, three quarters of a mile distant.

Grace's six older brothers and sisters were by now living on the mainland. A younger brother, William Brooks Darling, normally stationed in the lighthouse, happened also to be away at the time, working with the herring fishermen in the coastal village of North Sunderland.* His fortuitous absence was, as fate would have it, the proximate cause of his sister's subsequent fame.

With the help of Mrs Darling, Grace and her father launched their coble.** When the tide seemed favourable, Grace and Mr Darling each took an oar and set out for the Big Harcar, where Mr Darling leapt out of the coble and on to the rock while Grace stayed on the oars, rowing back

---

*Name later changed to Seahouses.
**'A short flat-bottomed rowing boat . . . used chiefly on the NE coast of England.' (*OED*)

Anonymous painting of the rescue, c.1845. Compare this with the frontispiece

View of Bamburgh Castle by
W. A. Nesfield, c.1832

and forth to prevent the boat from being dashed to pieces
on the treacherous reef.

They found nine survivors: four crew members and five
passengers including one woman, a Mrs Dawson, whose
small children had died in her arms of exposure and
injuries. Another passenger, a Revd Mr Cobb, had also
succumbed by the time the Darlings reached the rock.

As there was not room in the boat for all nine, Mr
Darling took on board Mrs Dawson, an injured crew
member, and three able-bodied men who would help row
while Grace attended to the injured. They successfully
returned to the Longstone where Grace, Mrs Dawson, and
two male passengers disembarked. Mr Darling and two of
the *Forfarshire* crew then rowed back to the Big Harcar to
bring off the remaining four.

The fishermen at North Sunderland had been alerted to
the wreck in the customary fashion, by repeated bursts of
gunfire from the lookout in Bamburgh Castle three miles
away. Six fishermen, accompanied by eighteen-year-old
William Brooks Darling, embarked for the five-mile row

Anonymous engraving of Grace and the survivors warming themselves in the Darlings' living-room in the Longstone Lighthouse

to the Big Harcar, but discovered on arrival only the bodies of the dead children and the clergyman.

As the weather was too rough to risk returning to the mainland, William Brooks directed his companions to the Longstone, where for three days a total of nineteen remained storm bound, crammed into the lighthouse and outbuildings.

The primary source, as historians would call it, for these events is *Darling's Journal*, a printed version of which is preserved in the Grace Darling Museum. The journal, which Mr Darling kept throughout his long tenure as lighthouse keeper, is not a diary but rather a log-book, a series of entries relating to his occupation: lists of fish and game caught; notes on the increasingly high cost of such mainland necessities as flour, corn, oatmeal; inventories of salvage recovered from the sea ('four logs timber 124

feet . . . they sold for £14 and I received for salvage £1 10s'.)
He makes no mention of the births of his many children,
nor of the death of his mother in 1813.

Like all English people, he is much preoccupied with
the weather, and the state of his garden: 'Severe gale or
hurricane from west . . . This summer, earwigs very
numerous in the garden. I caught frequently one quart on
the evening . . .' In the same laconic style, he reports on
numerous shipwrecks observed from the lighthouse and
his efforts to rescue survivors or retrieve salvage, usually
with the help of his sons.

In only one entry does he mention personal risk
encountered in the course of a rescue. This is dated 27
December 1834, four years before the *Forfarshire* wreck:

Wind S by E fresh gale. 11 p.m. The sloop *Autumn* of and to
Peterhead, with coals from Sunderland, struck east point of
Knavestone and immediately sank. Crew of three men; two
lost, one saved by the lightkeeper, and three sons, viz. William,
Robert and George, after a struggle of three hours. Having lost
two oars on the rock, had a very narrow escape.

PS. The man saved, James Logan, stood near ten hours, part on
the rock, part on the masthead; the mate lying dead beside him
on the rock the last three hours, having perished from cold.

In contrast, his account of the *Forfarshire* wreck and
rescue is a terse recital of facts about the steamship and its
cargo – there is no indication of danger, and no mention of
his daughter. (According to Mr Calderwell of the Grace
Darling Museum, when Mr Darling writes that nine 'were
rescued by the Darlings' he may have been referring to the
lighthouse coble which was known by that name.)

As in many another entry in his journal concerning
shipwrecks that entailed loss of life, this one is headed
'Melancholy':

1838   Melancholy
Sept[r] 7 – The steam-boat *Forfarshire*, 400 tons, sailed from
Hull for Dundee on the 6th, at midnight. When off Berwick, her
boilers became so leaky as to render the engine useless. Captain
Humble then bore away for Shields; blowing strong gale, north,
with thick fog. About 4 am on the 7th, the vessel struck the west
point of Harker's rock, and in fifteen minutes broke through by
the paddle-axle, and drowned forty three persons; nine having
previously left in their own boat, and were picked up by a

Montrose vessel, and carried to Shields, and nine others held on by the wreck and were rescued by the Darlings. The cargo consisted of superfine cloths, hardware, soap, boiler-plate and spinning gear.

Word of the shipwreck was slow to reach the public, as the gathering and dissemination of news in 1838 was a laborious and haphazard process. The telegraph was several years in the future, and there were as yet no trains to the north of England. The year 1838 was marked by the opening of the London–Birmingham railway, the northernmost point thus far for train travel from London, which thrilling event drew hundreds of spectators and inspired colourful accounts in newspapers throughout Britain. Steamships were just beginning to come into regular commercial use, the first transatlantic crossings having

Grace Darling and her father William going to the rescue – painting after J. W. Carmichael, c.1845

occurred in that same year. It was a year just on the eve of inventions and discoveries which would within a few decades change England's accustomed way of life.

Like steamships and trains, journalism in the sense of gathering news on the spot was a still-emerging phenomenon that gave rise to a new occupation: that of the 'penny-a-liner', who would grab whatever information or gossip he could find and then race by coach, horseback or ship to deliver his lines to his employer.*

For an event such as the wreck of the *Forfarshire*, London newspapers would rely entirely upon accounts in the northern press, which in turn would batten upon each other – the *Warder* of Berwick-on-Tweed quoting from the *Dundee Courier*, and so on, information that would eventually surface days later in *The Times*.

Charles Dickens (who was no penny-a-liner, but like his father before him a respectable parliamentary reporter) in 1865 gave a graphic account to a group of newspaper men of what it was like getting and delivering a story in the 1830s:

I have often transcribed for the printer, from my shorthand notes, important public speeches in which the strictest accuracy was required, and a mistake in which would have been to a young man extremely compromising, writing on the palm of my hand by the light of a dark lantern, in a post-chaise and four, galloping through a wild country, and through the dead of the night, at the then surprising rate of fifteen miles an hour. . . Returning home from exciting political meetings in the country to the waiting press in London, I verily believe I have been upset in almost every description of vehicle known in this country. I have been, in my time, belated on miry by-roads, towards the small hours, forty or fifty miles from London, in a wheelless

---

*The dismal lot of lower-rung journalists of the early nineteenth century can be glimpsed from this entry in the *Dictionary of National Biography* about a collateral forebear of mine, John Mitford (1782–1831):
'. . . Mitford was discharged from the navy as insane, and he took to journalism and strong drink . . . The publisher who employed him found that the only way to make him work was to keep him without money. He therefore limited him to a shilling a day, which Mitford expended on two pennyworth of bread and cheese and an onion, and the balance on gin. With this, and his day's supply of paper and ink, he repaired to an old gravel-pit in Battersea Fields, and there wrote and slept till it was time to take in his work and get his next shilling. . .'

carriage, with exhausted horses and drunken postboys, and have got back in time for publication, to be received with never-forgotten compliments by the late Mr Black, coming in the broadest Scotch from the broadest of hearts I ever knew.

Newspapers were uncommonly costly. For example, *The Times*, at fivepence a copy, would have been far out of reach for the average wage-earner. The news-hungry public relied largely on the broadside, or broadsheet, quickly and cheaply produced by local printers for sale in the streets and taverns. These consisted of a single large page of serried print, rushed out by low-paid labour on the newly invented mechanical press, for distribution in the town on the same day.

One of these, signed merely 'John Muir, Printer', gives details of the *Forfarshire* wreck so far as they could be ascertained as of 11 September, four days after the event. It illustrates both the difficulties encountered and the ingenuity required to make sense of the news as it filtered through from various sources. Muir's solution was to print excerpts, often contradictory, from half a dozen Scottish newspapers.

His opening paragraph, from the *Dundee Courier* of 11 September, dramatically conveys the grim atmosphere as the people of Dundee, where the *Forfarshire* was due to have docked, waited for the night mail. Nobody writes like this any longer, more's the pity:

Before the arrival of the mail at 11 o'clock a dense crowd collected in front of the post-office, among whom a death-like silence prevailed, testifying the interest which pervaded them as to the fate and crew of the *Forfarshire*. When the mail came up the guard announced, that a gentleman who had come to Edinburgh with the London mail instructed him to carry the intelligence to Dundee that 35 of the crew and passengers of the steam ship were drowned. This news being mere report the multitude waited in breathless anxiety for the declaration of the gentleman connected with the Hull Steam Packet Company then in the post-office. That declaration, we are sorry to say, more than confirmed their worst fears.

The gentleman from the Dundee & Hull Steam Packet Company, owners of the *Forfarshire*, furnished a list of the eight crew members and one passenger who had got away in the ship's boat, and he added that 'a boat was sent to the

(*over page*) 'SS Forfarshire Leaving Hull her Last Voyage' by John Ward, 1798–1849

vessel which brought the intelligence that other nine of the crew and passengers were saved: – 2 Firemen; a Carpenter; a Cook; a Woman, and 4 steerage passengers'. These were the survivors saved by Grace and her father, but there is as yet no mention of the Darlings' name in the press.

On 11 September, a coroner's jury was hastily convened in Bamburgh by Mr Robert Smeddle, a personage of great importance in those parts. He was secretary to the Crewe Trust, a charitable foundation housed in Bamburgh Castle that provided free schooling for children of the poor, an infirmary, and accommodation for shipwrecked sailors. It was he who had given the order to fire the alert from Bamburgh Castle when the *Forfarshire* wreck had been spotted at daybreak by a lookout, and who had ridden to North Sunderland to alert the fishermen to make the attempt to rescue survivors.

The purpose of a coroner's jury – then as now – is to determine the cause of death; in this case, the deaths of Mrs Dawson's children, the clergyman, and a few others whose bodies had fetched up since the wreck. But a coroner's jury, like any other, is not immune to prevailing community prejudice. Steamships were, to the tradition-bound folk of Northumberland, particularly suspect as an unwelcome newfangled invention of dubious worth compared to the stout sailing vessels that everybody was used to.

The *Forfarshire*, described by its owners as 'a splendid and powerful steam-vessel' of 'great propulsive force, as high if not higher than that of any steamer of the size now afloat' had been in service for only two years before the fatal wreck. Splendour was indeed the note. There were private staterooms for the very grand; a ladies' cabin and one for gentlemen; a deck for steerage passengers and 'excellent accommodation for horses, livestock, carriages, etc.'. Murals by a well-known artist of the day, Horatio McCulloch, adorned the saloons. Lavish meals were served on gilt-scrolled china, huge dinner plates inscribed with a likeness of the vessel, a few of which were salvaged and can still be seen in the Grace Darling Museum.

The London *Sun*'s 'Correspondent On The Spot' in North Sunderland described the 'intense and painful interest in this neighbourhood' occasioned by 'the

HULL & DUNDEE.

THE DUNDEE & HULL STEAM-PACKET COMPANY'S

SPLENDID AND POWERFUL STEAM-VESSEL

FORFARSHIRE,

450 Tons Burden, and 200 Horse-power,

CAPTAIN JAMES MONCRIEFF,

IS APPOINTED TO SAIL AS UNDER, WEATHER, &c., PERMITTING:

FROM HULL.			FROM DUNDEE.		
WEDNESDAY, 6 December, 10 *p.m.*			SATURDAY, 2 December, 11 *p.m.*		
„	13	„ 5 „	„	9	„ 10 „
„	20	„ 9 „	„	16	„ 11 „
„	27	„ 4 „	„	23	„ 10 „
1838.			„	30	„ 11 „
WEDNESDAY, 3 January, 9 „			1838.		
„	10	„ 4 „	SATURDAY, 7 January, 10 „		
„	17	„ 8 „	„	14	„ 11 „
„	24	„ 3 „	„	21	„ 10 „
„	31	„ 7 „	„	28	„ 11 „

FARES.

MAIN CABIN, ... £1, 5s.——**FORE CABIN,** . . . . . 15s.
DECK (Common Soldiers and Sailors), . . 7s. 6d.

Provisions, Wines, and Spirits, to be had on board, on very moderate terms.

Berths must be secured at the Company's Offices; and Passengers are requested to be in attendance half an hour before the advertised time of sailing.

Particulars as to Freight of Goods, Carriages, Live Stock, &c., by the FORFAR-SHIRE, which is extremely reasonable, may be had of WILLIAM JUST, Manager, Dundee; JOHN GARIE, Agent, Perth; or of

GEORGE CAMMELL,
AGENT, HULL,

18, *EAST SIDE THE HUMBER DOCK;*

By whom Goods intended for Shipment, *by this rapid and regular conveyance,* will be *carefully dispatched,* when *specially addressed* to his care.

NOVEMBER 1837. D. ANNAN, PRINTER, DUNDEE.

melancholy loss of life which has occurred by the wreck of the *Forfarshire* steam-boat', and he gave details of the financial position: 'One merchant has £4,000 insured on his goods, and the vessel is insured. The entire loss may be stated at £20,000. The number of lives lost may be assumed at 42.' (As no passenger list was recovered, the precise number drowned was never determined.)

Before the inquest eight of the nine rescued by the Darlings had been liberated from their involuntary three-day detention at the Longstone Lighthouse, having been fetched off on 10 September, as soon as the storm had abated. John Tulloch, ship's carpenter, stayed on as custodian of remains of the wreckage. The injured were being cared for in Bamburgh. Several crew members who had got away in the *Forfarshire* lifeboat had made their way from Shields to Bamburgh. Mr William Just, manager of the steamship company, had hurried down from Dundee with one of the company's directors to inspect the wreck. Curiously, none of these were called to testify at the inquest.

The only witnesses examined were three steerage passengers rescued by the Darlings, and the Bamburgh custom-house officer who had gone out to inspect what was left of the wreck. The passengers with one accord assigned blame to the leaky state of the boilers, hence to the captain for putting to sea knowing of this potential danger:

One of the witnesses, James Kelly, passenger, said that so conscious was he of the inefficiency of the boilers that he would have given all he was worth to be put on shore again before they left the Humber. He considered the vessel quite unseaworthy, and had he been the captain, he would have put back immediately after leaving Hull.   (*Warden*, 15 September 1838)

The star witness was one Daniel Donovan, who as a former ship's fireman had been given free passage on the *Forfarshire*. He described the leaking boilers in detail:

Before they left the Humber the boilers were discovered to be leaking very much; they were then not twenty miles from Hull. The captain and mate must have known of the circumstance. It was the duty of the engineman to report it. When the boiler first ran out there was nothing said about taking the vessel back to Hull, which might have been done very easily . . .

(Constance Smedley, *Grace Darling and Her Times*)

The jury thereupon returned their verdict on the cause of death: 'Wrecked on board the *Forfarshire* steam-packet by the imperfections of the boilers, and culpable negligence of the captain in not putting back to port. – Deodand* on the vessel, £100.'

Following the verdict, the London *Sun*'s correspondent observed that 'different opinions are entertained as to the cause of this disaster' and that 'the prevailing opinion is, that there has been some mismanagement, and perhaps some imperfections in the boilers ...' He cautioned, however, that 'it will be but justice to all parties to suspend judgement on this, until further and better information can be produced; and this becomes the more necessary at present, as the Coroner's inquiry did not embrace the very important statements of ... the crew who have escaped from the wreck'.

Readers with scant interest in the problems of boilers and stay-bolts in the early days of steamships – and their number must be legion – are advised to skip the next few pages. I, too, thought the subject pretty boring, and far afield from the story of Grace Darling; however, it happened that just as I was ploughing through interminable contemporary reports and expert opinions on the lethal shortcomings of boiler manufacture and woefully inadequate inspection, the explosion of the spacecraft Challenger was unfolding on television before my very eyes. The parallel seemed quite striking: in each case the use of a fairly new, much-touted technology, said by its promoters to be absolutely safe, followed by the unearthing of much evidence to the contrary, and then frantic attempts at cover-up by those responsible.

Substitute O rings for stay-bolts, NASA officials for the *Forfarshire* owners, and it's almost the same story.

The London *Sun*, 24 September 1838, reported 'alarm in the public mind ... confidence greatly shaken by the circumstances which have already come to light ... Even before ship left Humber a leak observed in one of the boilers...'

---

*'*Deodand*. A thing forfeited or to be given to God: spec. in English law, a personal chattel which, having been the immediate occasion of the death of a human being, was given to God as an expiatory offering, i.e., forfeited to the Crown ... abolished in 1846.' (*OED*)

The story continues:

Now, what short of infatuation could have induced the master of the vessel to proceed on the voyage after this discovery? Ought not common caution, to say nothing of the responsibility of having so many lives entrusted to his charge, to have dictated an immediate return to Hull, to have the leak repaired? But culpable as the conduct of the master – who had fallen a sacrifice to his own temerity – must be considered, he was not the only person to blame. The proprietors of the *Forfarshire* must come in for a very large share of condemnation. They were well aware that the boilers were defective, for it is stated that they had been 'of late in a *leaky state*'. . . Nay, it appears that so sensible were the owners of the inefficiency of these boilers, that they had ordered materials for new ones to be supplied. . . Now what earthly excuse can they allege for thus risking, and as it happened, throwing away the lives of so many persons? . . . It is, therefore, to their grasping and inhuman cupidity, in striving to squeeze the greatest possible quantity of work out of their old and unseaworthy materials, that this wholesale and lamentable loss of life is principally, if not entirely, to be attributed. . .

. . . a legislative remedy has become absolutely necessary . . .

For many days after the inquest, the newspapers gave extensive coverage to the problems of steamship boilers in general, and those of the *Forfarshire* in particular. The *Warder* of 15 September notes the need 'to ascertain whether or not the melancholy occurrence falls to be added to the long list of similar accidents which have occurred through insufficiency of the steam boilers . . .' Pointing out that the *Forfarshire*, in service for only two years, was 'reckoned in every respect a particularly strong vessel', the *Warder* describes the boiler-maker, Mr Peter Borrie of Aberdeen, as one 'whose experience and abilities seemed sufficiently to guarantee their safety'. If not the boilers, what then caused the disaster? 'It has been represented to us that the accident might have occurred, not through any defect in the boilers, but by one or more of the stay bolts by which the plates are fastened together having lost their hold, and left open the apertures through which the water issued . . .'

While the jurors' condemnation of Captain Humble for his 'culpable negligence' seems unnecessarily harsh – after all, he went down with his ship as captains are supposed to do, moreover 'with his wife in his arms' according to witnesses – their perception of the primary

Grace Darling and her father rescuing the survivors of the *Forfarshire* steamboat – painting after J. W. Carmichael, *c.*1845

cause of the wreck being 'imperfections of the boilers' must have been on target.

The shipowners, mindful of large financial stakes involved not only in the case of the *Forfarshire* but for the future of steamships in general, fought back through the agency of their manager Mr Just.

He marshalled depositions, from a surviving crew member to the effect that the boilers were regularly inspected, and if discovered to be faulty were immediately repaired by the management, and from the foreman of the boiler-maker's factory, who swore that the *Forfarshire* boilers were in excellent condition as of the time he inspected them in Dundee on 25 August, a few days before the disaster.

Mr Just released these affidavits to the local newspapers which published them in full, together with his own letter to the *Dundee Chronicle* of 25 September, in which he deplores the premature closing of the inquest and the coroner's failure to call as witnesses the company directors, who would have testified to the soundness of the vessel, her boilers, and the company's rectitude in overseeing these matters.

This early exercise in public relations – manipulating opinion through use of the press – evidently paid off. Eventually, after four more bodies from the wreck were cast on shore, requiring the convening of another coroner's jury, a second inquest was held on 14 October, five weeks after the wreck. This afforded Mr Just the opportunity to present his company's position through the evidence of John Tulloch, ship's carpenter and one of those rescued by the Darlings.

Tulloch testified that there was nothing wrong with the boilers, which had been repaired before the *Forfarshire* left Hull; that he 'considered the hull and machinery to be good, seaworthy, and in good working order' and that 'the Captain was a steady, trustworthy man'. The jury, after ten minutes' deliberation, brought in a verdict that 'the deceased had been casually and accidentally drowned when on the high seas on board of the *Forfarshire* steamer, which vessel was wrecked in consequence of tempestuous weather'.

Coincidentally with Mr Just's efforts to gather evidence exonerating his employers, which took some weeks, Mr Crighton, the Surveyor of Shipping for Lloyd's in Dundee, wrote to the *Dundee Courier* (13 September 1836) with his version of where the fault lay. His letter begins with the usual obligatory reference to the tragedy:

SIR,

The melancholy occurrence of the loss of the steamer *Forfarshire* has created the most intense excitement throughout this town and neighbourhood, and the deepest sympathy in the fate of the numerous sufferers and their connections by this heart-rending calamity.

He proceeds to the point of his letter, which is that 'There are rumours abroad, which, if correct, tend greatly to aggravate this deplorable loss of life and property.'

In essence, Lloyd's own rules and regulations, requiring an examination and report on every vessel afloat, and that 'all vessels navigated by steam shall be surveyed at least twice each year and their condition carefully reported', were generally disregarded by the steamship companies.

Since the *Forfarshire* had left port without Lloyd's certificate of seaworthiness, Mr Crighton disclaims any responsibility for the melancholy occurrence:

A regard to my official capacity as Surveyor of Shipping for this port has induced me to trouble you with the above remarks that the public may be aware of the fact that I have never declined the performance of my duty when permitted or requested by ship-owners or agents; but I have no power to obtrude myself.

It is, unfortunately, a bit late to get to the bottom of it all. If the *Sunday Times* Insight team in England, or '60 Minutes' in America, had been in Bamburgh in 1838, they would doubtless have sprung about with their trusty tape-recorders interviewing all the principals involved in the drama of the boilers, the stay-bolts, the wreck and its aftermath. I can hear them now: 'Mr Just refused to be interviewed on camera . . .' Pan to Mr Borrie, boiler-maker of Aberdeen. Mr Borrie describes his fine boilers and suggests the stay-bolts might have been deficient. Pan to Mr Crichton of Lloyd's who reads from his letter of 13 September to the *Dundee Courier*:

It is evident to every person versant with nautical matters that a steamer with her engines disabled is the most helpless craft in a storm that can float upon the ocean: her paddles which give her such velocity when all is in right working order, become the most insuperable barriers to her making any headway under canvas and leave her to the mercy of the elements.

About now, viewers have got the general idea, which is that Mr Just managed to whitewash his company but stonewalled when asked to elaborate; that the boiler-maker blamed the stay-bolt maker; that Lloyd's man had a good point. Bored with boilers and stay-bolts, they switch to another channel. There is still no mention of Grace Darling.

With one accord, the eight crew members who got away in the *Forfarshire* lifeboat, abandoning all but one of the passengers to their fate, refuse all offers of television appearances. They have suffered enough opprobrium from the newspapers, which from the outset focused much attention on their unseemly behaviour.

Thus the *Sunday Times* of 16 September, quoting from the *Tyne Mercury*:

About a quarter of an hour before she struck, the crew, whose conduct was unlike that which is a characteristic of British seamen, lowered the larboard quarter boat down, and left the ship, the mate accompanying them, one passenger only succeeding in leaping into the boat . . .

The *Warder* of 15 September ran a 'declaration' attested to by the ship's engineer and first mate (copied from the *Dundee Courier*) offering the rather wet explanation that

the first mate states that when he left the vessel, no passenger, with the exception of Mr Ruthven Ritchie, wished to come off, although they saw them putting off the boat; and that another boat good was left.

The same issue carries a rhyme of eight verses by one of those instant poets whose work so often embellished the news of the day, signed only W. R. B. Considering that it must have been hurriedly dashed off, it is actually rather good:

The sea bird screamed o'er the faithless deep,
And wild was the note of her sorrow;
She seemed to bode that many should weep
The fate of the barque on the morrow.

But the steamer dashed gaily o'er wave and swell,
The foaming billows lashing;
The thoughtless sung, while the sick and grave
Marked the swift paddles' whirl and splashing.

The next several verses speculate about the crew's fears as they passed 'muddy Humber's tide', 'Tynemouth's mouldering walls', etc. The dénouement:

And was there alas! no boat save one,
And to that did the false crew hurry;
And of all the *passengers* was there none
Left to tell the sad mournful story?

They sank to their last and endless sleep
Just warned, and, in their beds confiding; –
A shriek was heard as they sank in the deep,
While away the false crew were gliding!

The *Shipping & Mercantile Gazette* (London, 20 September, quoting from the *Edinburgh Evening Post*, undated) berates the captain and the shipowners for their culpable negligence, but reserves its chief ire for the crew who, it is suggested, should be prosecuted for murder:

. . . the crew were allowed to seize the boat. When the boat was launched, the crew should have been the last to take advantage of it; instead of which they exclusively took possession of it . . .

. . . seamen found to desert their vessel, seizing the only means of escape, as these seamen have done, should be liable to punishment, precisely as if they had caused the murders which they left inevitable.

No doubt to the relief of the false crew, they soon glided into obscurity, forgotten by press, rhymesters, and public as news of Grace Darling's heroic act, first seized upon by a few northern newspapers, reached London and began to reverberate throughout the land.

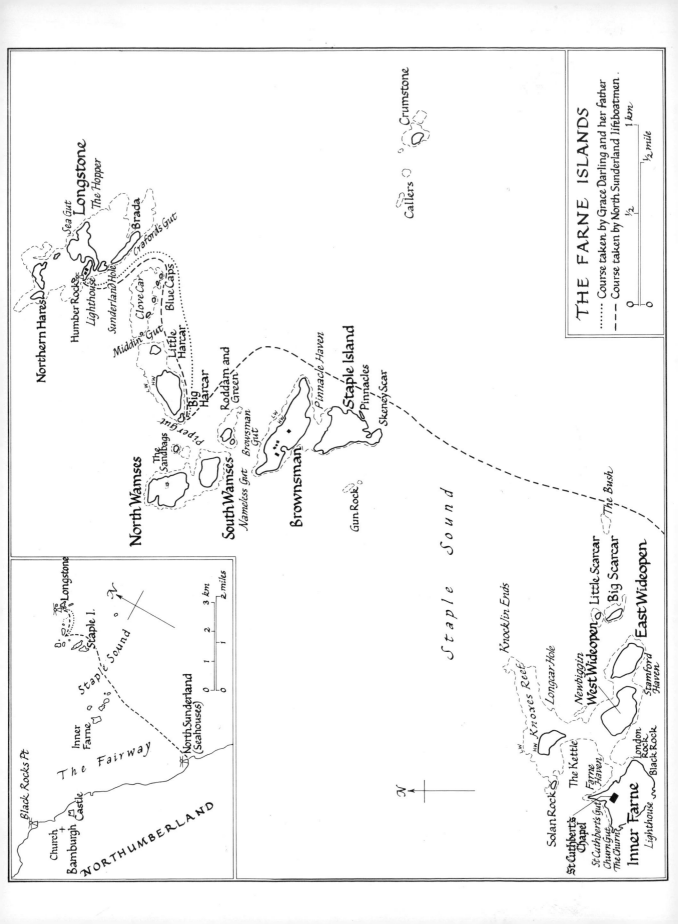

THE FARNE ISLANDS

.... Course taken by Grace Darling and her father
– – – – Course taken by North Sunderland lifeboatmen.

Crumstone

Callers

Longstone
Sea Gut
The Hopper
Humber Rock
Lighthouse
Sunderland Hole
Brada
Craford's Gut
Clove Car
Blue Caps
Northern Hares
Middin Gut
Little Harcar
Big Harcar
Roddam and Green
Piper's Gut
The Sandbags
North Wamses
Browsman Gut
Nameless Gut
South Wamses
Pinnacle Haven
Staple Island
Pinnacles
Skeney Scar
Brownsman
Gun Rock

Staple Sound

Knocklin Ends
Longcar Hole
Knoxes Reef
Newbiggin
West Wideopen
Little Scarcar
Big Scarcar
East Wideopen
Stamford Haven
The Bush
The Kettle
Farne Haven
London Rock
Black Rock
Solan Rock
St Cuthbert's Chapel
St Cuthbert's Gut
Churn Gut
The Churn
Inner Farne
Lighthouse

Black Rocks Pt
Church
Bamburgh Castle
NORTHUMBERLAND
Inner Farne
The Fairway
Longstone
Staple I.
Staple Sound
North Sunderland
(Seahouses)

0   1   2   3 km
0   1   2 miles

½   ½ mile
1 km

3. INTIMATIONS OF IMMORTALITY

The Northumbrian newspapers showed the way, and set the tone, for the celebration of Grace Darling and her Deed. As was then customary, their accounts were eventually picked up and reprinted – with or without attribution – by newspapers around the country, setting in motion an avalanche of hyperbolic acclaim for the lighthouse heroine that would sweep on down the nineteenth century, and well into the twentieth.

One of the first of these northern pace-setters was the *Warder* of Berwick-on-Tweed. In its edition of 15 September 1838 this excellent newspaper devoted several pages to a detailed report of the wreck, the inquest of 11 September, a list of those presumed dead, letters from the first mate, the passenger Ritchie, etc., printed verbatim; and, as we have seen, a poem castigating the false crew.

Somewhere in the middle of this extensive coverage occurs the following:

And here it is our gratifying duty to record an effort made for the rescue of the unfortunate sufferers by two individuals whose heroism, we are warranted in asserting, never was exceeded in any similar case, and is of so extraordinary a character, that had we not heard its truth attested by those who were benefited by it, we could not have been induced to give it our belief, ranking, as it does, amongst the noblest instances of purely disinterested and philanthropic exertion in behalf of suffering individuals that ever reflected honour upon humanity.

The writer here pauses for breath to describe the lighthouse, and continues:

The keeper of this lighthouse, — Darling, is one of the two individuals who have so honourably distinguished themselves, the other being Grace Darling, his daughter, a young woman of twenty-two years of age! . . . The latter, prompted by an impulse of heroism which in a female transcends all praise, seeing that it would have done honour to the stoutest hearted of the male sex, *urged her father to go off in the boat at all risks, offering herself to take one oar if he would take the other!* [Italics in the original.]

An editorial in the same edition calls for legislation placing official inspectors in every port to examine the condition of boilers and machinery in all steamships, and for punishment of shipowners who disregard the inspectors' regulations. It denounces the *Forfarshire* owners for 'extreme culpability, if not criminality' in sending the ship to sea 'with boilers in a condition so defective as hers evidently were'. It concludes:

But, we cannot close these remarks without alluding to the noble feelings, and heroic conduct of Grace Darling and her father, standing in bold relief, as they do, to the craven and unseamanlike desertion of a part of the crew . . . The humanity and fortitude of those two respectable individuals is beyond all praise; and cannot fail to bring down upon them warm thanks and blessings, if not more substantial marks of approbation.

For London readers, the first account of Grace Darling's heroic exploit appeared in *The Times* of 19 September 1838, twelve days after the rescue. In several earlier editions *The Times* had published news of the wreck and survivors copied from the northern newspapers, the most detailed of which, quoting from the *Tyne Mercury*, came out on 16 September. It is couched in the rich, beautiful prose of the penny-a-liner, no doubt writing with a view to increasing his pay by a few pence:

Since the report reached here on Saturday afternoon [i.e., eight days after the wreck] the most contradictory statements have been made respecting the loss of the *Forfarshire* . . . we regret to state that the true particulars have realized our worst fears, about thirty-eight individuals having met a watery grave; many of them were in bed at the time the vessel struck, and only rose to meet the cold embrace of death, as they sank beneath the angry and foaming waves.

The watery grave, the cold embrace of death, the angry and foaming waves may have earned an extra twopence, with another penny for the wreck itself, '. . . hurrying into another world the captain and nearly all his ill-fated companions'.

Once in a while, the assiduous reporter would achieve a scoop in the shape of a real interview with a real person – no matter that the informant got *his* information at second hand. These forerunners of UPI, AP, and Reuters established the pattern, followed to this day, of the knowledgeable though unnamed source, inspiring the reader's confidence in the accuracy of the story:

We have seen the driver of the Royal Williams coach [continues the *Tyne Mercury* correspondent] who is acquainted with some particulars, acquired principally from passengers who have travelled by the coach . . .

The writer gives these particulars at some length, and adds that 'The coachman said it was reported a woman had been saved from the wreck, but it was estimated that thirty-five or thirty-eight had perished.'

There are approximately 120 lines in this verbose news item, of which I have quoted only a fragment. The reporter would have been paid ten shillings at the going rate; but he unfortunately missed the scoop of the year, which appeared three days later in *The Times* over the signature of 'M.S.', datelined Morpeth, Northumberland, 15 September.

A newspaper from a bygone day, whatever its vintage – last month's, last year's, or last century's – has the uncanny effect of transporting the reader backwards in time to the date of its publication; a magic-carpet exercise in which we get caught up in the concerns of that day, the latest news, irate letters-to-editor, reviews of current books and plays, all as fresh and urgent as though it had only happened yesterday – which, of course, it had.

Searching through *The Times* of 19 September 1838 for M.S.'s account of Grace Darling, I found myself in just such a time-warp, hopelessly sidetracked, mesmerized by other fascinating items. This vast newspaper of eight pages measuring almost two by one-and-a-half feet (21 × 16 in, to be exact) is set in such minuscule, eye-straining type that one can hardly scan, or browse through it; it requires painstaking, line-by-line concentration to get the full flavour.

The first two pages consist entirely of classified

advertisements – a format adhered to by *The Times* until 1966, when the editor reluctantly capitulated to the modern custom, long adopted by his competitors, of printing the news of the day up front.

Cost of the advertisements was fairly cheap: five shillings for up to four lines, and sixpence for each extra line. *The Times* did not solicit advertising, but relied upon its high circulation to attract it. The issue of 19 September 1838 carried 517 ads. Conversely, the ads themselves may have attracted readers. I found them so beguiling, so vibrant with immediacy that I longed to find out more about the advertiser, the responses, the outcome – almost forgetting that all are long since beneath the sod:

WANTED A YOUTH, in a wholesale warehouse in the city. No salary will be given the first year. Apply by letter to Y.Z., 28 Watling street.

Printing newspapers in the nineteenth century: engravings of a compositor at work, 1833,

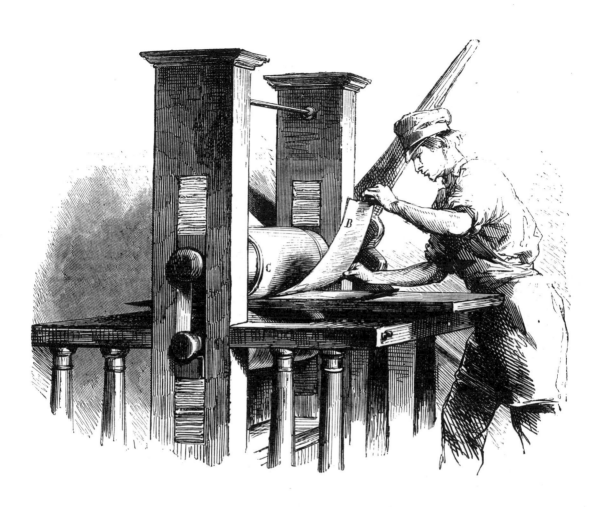

and a copperplate press being
operated

Poor lad! But the next employer is more generous:

WANTED, in a small family, residing at Peckham-on-Rye, a
respectable young woman, as NURSE, whose character will bear
strict enquiry as to capability and general conduct. Wages 10
guineas a year, to be raised to 12. Personal application to be
made to-morrow, the 20th inst. . . .

Half of page 3, the first news page, is devoted to an
unsigned review of a new translation of 'The Clouds of
Aristophanes, with Notes Critical and Explanatory, by T.
Mitchell, AM'. It is on the whole what publishers call a
'selling review'; T. Mitchell must be so pleased, I thought,

with the unqualified praise of his scholarship and 'delicate euphony', although the last paragraph contains these strictures: 'One word more, and we have done. It is not often that we notice typographical inaccuracies; but the errata in the text of this play, and in the notes subjoined to it, are so numerous as to require animadversion . . .'

Where have I read this sort of thing before? In the *New York Review* – or the *London Review – of Books*; although I do not recall much use of 'animadversion' in those august publications.

The news on page 3 is given in no particular order. Following Aristophanes I read:

EXTRAORDINARY PHENOMENON
(From a correspondent) – At half-past 7 o'clock last Sunday evening, there was observed at St Alban's, the sky being perfectly clear and star-light, a bright band of light, extending from about 20 degrees from the western horizon to about 40 degrees from the eastern horizon. . . It then moved very slowly towards the south, where it remained stationary till, in about a quarter of an hour, it had gradually disappeared . . .' [UFO watchers, please take note.]

There is much more on page 3 that holds my attention: 'PROLIFIC WHEAT', describing a new variety, how it should be sown, etc.; a long interrogation of a church-warden about the disappearance of some account books; and an item about the 'splendid exhibition and fête' at the Windsor and Eton Royal Horticultural Society. This was visited by the Queen, mounted on her 'favourite grey charger, with a number of led horses, attended by grooms in the Royal Livery'. After she had 'for a few minutes entered into conversation with her illustrious mother, the Queen of the Belgians, Lord Melbourne, etc., . . . Her Majesty returned at a very slow pace and reached the Castle at 20 minutes past 4 o'clock'.

I was further distracted from Grace Darling by the editorials on page 4, the first of which is a leader beginning:

The iniquity of the foreign policy of France, which has so suddenly burst forth within a few months, assumes on every side so fearful and identical a character, that our columns hardly suffice to enumerate the variety of her designs or of the means she has recourse to in their execution.

At issue, it seems, is a treaty with the Emir of Turkey in which the Emir 'acknowledges the sovereignty of France in Africa' with a view to binding the Emir against the interests of England.

Next is a lengthy blast against a letter from Daniel O'Connell, addressed to the people of Ireland, enumerating grievances and proposing electoral reform:

When we look back at the whole result of the letter to the Irish . . . we confess that even our long experience of Hibernian gullibility in general, and of the learned writer's individual audacity, does not save us from a feeling near akin to astonishment. We cannot altogether excuse a sensation of wonder, that he should venture to halloo his wild people on . . .

It was almost a relief to turn from the hectoring, sabre-rattling leaders to a lengthy account of a magnificent ball given in Milan – and to learn that 'the Paris papers of Monday have reached us by the ordinary express, but contain little news of interest'.

Best of all is the crime reporting, in the lurid style of the *News of the World* in England or, in America, the *National Enquirer*, with many a vivid word-picture of witnesses and accused:

Greenwood, a big, rough, redheaded man, was called on behalf of the prosecutrix . . .

Mr Norris . . . stated that the defendant was the most violent ruffian amongst the troop of drivers and cads in the neighbourhood . . .

Joseph Sinfield, labourer, aged 24, a heavy, dull-looking fellow . . .

Almost invariably, the accused is found guilty. Occasionally the judge is magnanimous, as in the case of William Jones, labourer, aged thirteen, indicted for stealing a snuff-box. The jury found him guilty, 'but as he did not appear to be previously known as a pickpocket, he was sentenced to be imprisoned and kept to hard labour for three months only'.

Conversely Mary Smith, convicted of stealing a wedding-ring worth ten shillings, is 'sentenced to be transported for the term of seven years'.

There is worse in store for Alfred Armstrong, a labourer aged twenty-one, indicted with a confederate, Joseph Roots, for stealing a sheep valued at twenty-five shillings. Armstrong, who had told friends that he had some mutton for sale, proffers the rather lame defence that the alleged sheep was in fact venison, not mutton; but this is refuted by a butcher who gives evidence that he had inspected the carcase, which was indeed a sheep.

The prisoners are found guilty, giving the judge an opening to lecture them on both the gravity of their crime and on their good fortune in that the penalty for sheep stealing had lately been modified:

Mr SERJEANT Arabin said, that the offence of which the prisoners had been convicted, although, fortunately for them, no longer capital, was still of a very serious description, and he regretted to add, that it was increasing in the country. The prisoners must therefore expect to be sent out of the country for a long time ...

whereupon he sentences Roots to be transported for ten years, and Armstrong for fifteen.

Armstrong has the last word: 'the latter on leaving the dock said, "Good 'by, my Lord."'

And finally, I reach my goal: Grace Darling. She appears towards the end of M.S.'s exhaustive report of the 11 September inquest and its outcome. He introduces her in these words:

Connected with this, the most calamitous case of shipwreck perhaps that has occurred since the loss of the *Rothsay Castle* off the Isle of Anglesea, is an instance of heroism and intrepidity on the part of a female unequalled perhaps, certainly not surpassed, by any on record. I allude to the heroic conduct of Miss Grace Horsley Darling ... The cries of the sufferers on the remaining part of the wreck were heard during the night by this female, who immediately awakened her father.

He describes their discovery at daybreak that people were moving on the rock, the launching of the boat by 'the old man'* and 'his intrepid daughter', and how 'they

Anonymous portrait of Grace Darling

*Mr Darling was aged fifty-three at the time, but is characterized in this and all subsequent accounts as 'old', 'venerable', 'her aged father', etc. A trace of ageism here?

In order to arrive at any thing like a correct idea of the danger of the undertaking, and of the fortitude and disinterestedness of the individuals who encountered and overcame it, at the imminent risk of their own lives, let the reader reflect for a little on the attendant circumstances. On every hand danger presented itself in a thousand terrific forms. The ocean, lashed by the tempest into the most tumultuous commotion, presented a barrier which would have seemed to all but those two intrepid persons wholly insurmountable by human energy. Again, on the other hand, there was no hope of reward—no encouraging plaudit, to stimulate to brave exertions, or to awaken emulation. Nothing but the pure and ardent wish to save the sufferers from impending destruction could have induced those two individuals to enter upon so perilous an expedition, fraught as it was with the imminent hazard of their own lives. Surely, imagination in its loftiest creations never invested the female character with such a degree of fortitude as has been evinced by Miss Grace Horsley Darling on this occasion. Is there in the whole field of history, or of fiction even, one instance of female heroism to compare for one moment with this?

The names of the individuals saved from the wreck of the

succeeded, after many ''hairbreadth 'scapes'' in navigating their frail skiff over the foaming billows . . .', and how when Mr Darling landed on the rock the 'frail boat' was 'kept afloat by the skilfulness and dexterity of his noble-minded daughter, who is said to be of slender appearance'.

Arrived back at the lighthouse,

Comment on the rescue in *The Times*, 19 September 1838

the same tender hand that had been so eminently instrumental in preserving them from a watery grave anxiously for three days and nights waited on the sufferers, administered to their wants, and soothed their afflictions. It is impossible to speak in adequate terms of the unparalleled bravery and disinterestedness shown on this occasion by Mr Darling and his truly heroic daughter, especially so with regard to the latter. Surely such unexampled heroism will not go unrewarded.

M.S. is approaching his peroration. He exhorts the reader to 'reflect for a little on the attendant circumstances' –

danger in 'a thousand terrific forms . . . the ocean lashed by the tempest into the most tumultuous condition . . .' 'the pure and ardent wish to save the sufferers from impending destruction . . .' and he winds up:

Surely, imagination in its loftiest creations never invested the female character with such a degree of fortitude as has been evinced by Miss Grace Horsley Darling on this occasion. Is there in the whole field of history, or of fiction even, one instance of female heroism to compare for one moment with this?

A strangely similar story had appeared a week earlier in the *Newcastle Chronicle*, containing many identical phrases: '. . . kept afloat by the skilfulness and dexterity of this noble-minded young woman', etc. The *Newcastle Chronicle* has this addition: 'One of the old seamen was moved to tears when he saw a young female of slender appearance perilling her life for their preservation.' (These tears continued to flow, as in this account published in 1842 in *Local Historian's Table Book* by M. A. Richardson: 'This perilous achievement – unexampled in the feats of female fortitude – was witnessed by the survivors in silent wonder – and down the weather-beaten cheek of one old seaman stole the big round tear when he beheld from the wreck the noble exertions of a young female of slender appearance . . .')

Although M.S. was not the first to spring the story of Grace Darling's heroic exploit upon a waiting world – for as we have seen, he was preceded by the northern press – it was surely his account in *The Times* that introduced her to the capital and thence to the nation as a whole. In that sense he should be credited as the principal creator of the legend, the granddaddy from whose pioneering panegyric flowed the subsequent torrent of poems, songs, books about Grace and her Deed. Thus all, including the present writer, who have embarked on an account of Grace Darling are to some extent in debt to M.S.

What manner of man was he, how much did *The Times* pay him for the story? Did he have other jobs aside from freelance writing, always the most precarious of livelihoods? His employer, I thought, must have the answers, so I rang up *The Times* expecting that somebody there would have at their fingertips everything that could be known about this valuable reporter. The switchboard operator had never heard of him, so she referred me to the archivist. The archivist imparted the dire news that some unknown philistine in *The Times*'s management had destroyed all personnel records prior to 1847, possibly because they were taking up too much space. She wasn't sure, as any memoranda explaining this act of vandalism would themselves have been put to the torch – precursor of the shredder.

As to remuneration, the archivist said that in general fees were paid according to the circulation of the newspaper, and that the going rate at *The Times* for somebody like M.S. was probably still a penny a line in 1838. As it was common for reporters to sell their stories to more than one newspaper, M.S. would likely have sent his to the *Newcastle Chronicle* – accounting for the identical phrases in both newspapers.

If M.S. is irrevocably lost in the mists of antiquity (as he himself might put it), all record of him obliterated by a penurious, space-saving forerunner of Mr Murdoch, at least one should be able to discover something about his occupation: the day-to-day regime of the penny-a-liner, how he was compensated, how he lived.

There are countless books and articles on the history of journalism, including a four-volume history of *The Times*, but these deal almost entirely with high-level editorial policy, the shifting relationships of editors with the government of the day and the like. They are not concerned with the humdrum affairs of the drudges who gathered the daily news. An exception is *The Newspaper Press: Its Origin, Progress and Present Position* by James Grant, published in 1871.* Mr Grant, himself for many years editor of the London *Morning Advertiser*, devotes an informative and entertaining chapter to the penny-a-liners, many of whom he had dealings with in his role as editor. He clearly appreciated and enjoyed their special qualities:

Amidst all the drudgery which penny-a-liners have to go through, there is a wonderful buoyancy, mingled with humour, in some of their number. The life they lead is one of great excitement, and that seems to keep their spirits up.

---

*London: Tinsley Brothers, 18 Catherine Street, Strand.

GRACE DARLING,

OR,

THE WRECK.

NARRATIVE BALLAD.

WRITTEN AND ADAPTED TO THE AIR "THE BOATIE ROWS,"

BY

CHRISTOPHER THOMSON.

About a mile from the rock on which the Forfarshire struck, is situated the Fern Lighthouse, kept by Mr. Darling, one of the individuals who so honourably distinguished themselves in the rescue of the unfortunate sufferers, the other being Grace Darling, his daughter, a young woman, of 22 years of age. The heroism of these two individuals is of so extraordinary a character that, had we not heard its truth attested by those who were preserved by it, we could not have been induced to give it our belief, ranking as it does amongst the many noble instances of purely disinterested and philanthropic exertions, in behalf of the suffering individuals, that ever reflected honour upon humanity. The thrill of delight which the survivors experienced when they saw the boat rowing round the south end of the rock towards themselves, was converted into a feeling of amazement which they could not find language to give expression to, when they became aware that one of their deliverers was a female. Health, honour, and happiness to that female! and may all this world's prosperity attend upon the steps of GRACE HORSLEY DARLING.—*The Public Recorder.*

[Ent. Sta. Hall.]   [Price 2s.]

London:

PUBLISHED FOR THE PROPRIETOR, BY Z. T. PURDAY, 45, HIGH HOLBORN.

Printed by R. E. LEE, at the "RECORDER" Office, Boswell Court, Temple Bar.

This curious subspecies of the genus newspaperman is long extinct; today, his nearest equivalent might be the 'stringer', meaning a part-time reporter stationed out of town or abroad who files with his employer such stories as happen to arise in his vicinity. But unlike the stringer, who generally supplements his payment for news items with other jobs, the 'liner' as he was called for short in the trade had no other source of income. His life was one of total, single-minded dedication to his work.

He spent his days rushing from place to place, often walking six or seven miles a day in search of news; his evenings preparing his copy; and his nights delivering it to the morning papers in time to meet their deadline. His prime sources were coroners' inquests, likely to yield stories of violent deaths and suicides, and fires, to this day favourite news subjects, as those of us who tune in to our local television news hour can affirm.

Having got the story, the next step for the London-based liner was to make copies for his clients, the sub-editors of the six morning papers. This must have required considerable technical skill. Using sheets of flimsy paper interspersed with 'blackened' paper, an early version of carbon paper, he wrote with a piece of ivory tapered to a sharp point, thus producing simultaneously six impressions of his report. Six was in fact the maximum number of copies that could be legibly produced by this method; no matter how hard he bore down with his ivory tip, a seventh or eighth would be so faint as to be hardly readable.

By the time all this was accomplished it might be midnight or later, with the final, crucial task still ahead: delivery of the copy to each newspaper office, in a special letterbox made accessible all night for the purpose.

At the end of this gruelling day of unremitting labour, the liner might – or might not – make a few shillings, depending on the sub-editor's estimate of the newsworthiness of his copy. Grant, assuming the pay to have risen to a penny-halfpenny a line, gives this example: the liner sells 40 lines for 5s. If three papers out of the six use his copy, he makes 15s. If he could average this sum for four days a week, he would get an aggregate of £3. If he could earn £3 a week the year round, he would get on pretty well because his needs were minimal; he was not expected to dress or live like Parliamentary reporters, who had to 'make an appearance'.

Two portraits of Grace Darling by H. P. Parker, 1838

Portrait of Grace's father by H. P. Parker, 1838

Portrait of Grace's mother by H. P. Parker, 1838

View of Bamburgh by T. Sutherland, after T. M. Richardson, 1820

(left) Items of Grace's clothing, including fragments of the clothes she wore during the rescue (see case at rear) – Grace Darling Museum

(top) 'Wreck of the *Forfarshire* steamer on one of the rocks of the Ferne Islands as it appeared at daybreak on the morning of 7th September 1838' by Leitch, from a drawing by J. W. Carmichael

(right) Portrayal of the rescue by William Bell Scott: part of a series of panels illustrating events in Northumbrian history which were painted between 1856 and 1860 to decorate the Central Hall in Wallington. According to the National Trust's brochure in Wallington, Bell Scott shared many of the ideals of the Pre-Raphaelite Brotherhood: 'immense care was taken with all the details, as one of the principal Pre-Raphaelite precepts was truth'. If this is the case, one wonders what the baby is doing in the rescue scene.

(over page) The Farne Islands today in more clement conditions.

Pottery inspired by Grace Darling laid out on a paisley shawl that belonged to her
– Grace Darling Museum

The latest thing in Grace Darling
artefacts: a 1987 Royal Doulton
statuette in which Grace, with
abundant, shoulder-length black
hair, is transformed into a
composite of Elizabeth Taylor and
Snow White

Offer for a Grace Darling statuette appearing on a Captain Morgan Rum bottle. Note that the bottle itself shows a replica of the medallion awarded to Grace Darling for her bravery

Grace Darling window at
Bamburgh church

Photograph of Grace Darling's
tomb, reconstructed in 1885

In their scramble for scoops the liners used all sorts of ingenious ruses. One took lodgings above a fire station so that he would be on hand at any moment of the day or night to dash out with the firemen and arrive on the scene long before any other liner could have heard of the fire. He had his stories all written and copied out on 'flimsy' in advance, leaving gaps for the place and time of the 'terrible conflagration', the extent of damage done and the numbers who 'perished in a fiery death', so that he could deliver his copy to several editors immediately after the event. (The gaps were easily filled in, for as Grant observes 'the same description will answer in the main for the great majority of fires'.) As a result of his clever living arrangements, this particular liner cornered the market on press coverage of fires, and for years held a virtual monopoly on the desirable fire beat, to the envy of his competitors.

Perilously balanced on the edge of poverty, and forced by the nature of his calling to work insanely long hours, what impelled the liner to persist in his miserable occupation? For according to Grant, few dropped out and many even induced their sons to enter 'the same "profession" – the name with which they dignify their reports of fires, inquests, and other exciting occurrences'.

Possibly the liner, like other writers, found his true reward in the very act of creative composition. His objectives were twofold: to catch the sub-editor's eye in this highly competitive field by using the most dramatic and lurid opening words he could think of, and to stretch out his story to the maximum possible length in order to garner extra pennies for his day's work.

This part must have been great fun to do, an exercise in ingenuity and speed – perhaps it compensated for the boredom of the inquests and other events he covered during the day, and for the drudgery of the night-time deliveries to come. In the liner's soaring prose, a common suicide would become 'The most desperate case of suicide ever known', throwing whole towns into 'utmost misery and consternation'. As a good specimen of the liner's artistic approach to his subject-matter, Grant cites this headline in a simple case of sudden death:

'AWFULLY SUDDEN DEATH OF A LATE CUSTOM-HOUSE OFFICER'S ELDEST SON IN A PORK-BUTCHER'S SHOP.'

THE LOSS

OF THE

STEAMSHIP

FORFARSHIRE,

CAPTAIN HUMBLE,

Which Struck on the Fern Islands

On her Voyage to Dundee, on the night of the 7th September, 1838, and

THE HEROIC CONDUCT

OF

GRACE DARLING,

*In venturing her life, and rescuing the Survivors from
destruction.*

SOLD BY ALL BOOKSELLERS.

What editor could resist? the writer must have asked himself, as he pressed away on the flimsies with his ivory stick to parley his report of the event into no less than thirty-two richly rewarding lines.

Once sensitized to the *modus vivendi* of the liner and the highly specialized prose style that he perforce developed, the reader has only to look through any newspaper of the period to find examples. While searching for additional Grace Darling stories I came across this, reproduced here line for line exactly as printed in *The Times* of 22 October 1838, with an attribution to 'Hertford paper':

> Sunday morning, as the Rev. S. Hillyard, the
> venerable minister of the Old Meeting-House, Bedford, was
> about to conclude his sermon, he was suddenly seized with a
> fainting fit, and sank down insensible. One of his friends
> was instantly in the pulpit and raised him up, when he soon
> recovered his consciousness. Mr. Blower, the surgeon, was
> immediately sent for, and arrived in about five minutes, when
> Mr. Hillyard was removed to Mr. Blower's house, and thence
> in a fly to his own dwelling. As the rev. gentleman has had
> two or three attacks of a paralytic nature, the congregation
> generally thought this was another, and probably a fatal one:
> the confusion and consternation which ensued when they saw
> their respected pastor fall was such as it is impossible to
> describe. Mr Hillyard is better, and now merely suffering
> from weakness, which it is hoped is but temporary.
> *Hertford paper.*

This comes out to fifteen lines, for which the liner would have been paid 1s. 3d. from *The Times*, plus something from 'Hertford paper' – and, of course, additional pence if he was able to place it elsewhere. Today, this non-news item, if thought worthy of report at all, might read 'Revd S. Hillyard of Bedford is recovering from a brief illness.'

While the chronicler of the Revd S. Hillyard's fainting spell may have had a little trouble spinning out his account to a satisfactorily remunerative length, M.S. and his contemporaries on the trail of Grace Darling should have had no such difficulty. Her story was the perfect vehicle for the liner's distinctive art; seldom can subject matter and writer's style have been so well-matched.

MISS GRACE HORSLEY DARLING.

Our readers must have observed constant references to the name of *Grace Darling*, in the newspapers, for several months past, and most of them, no doubt, are familiar with the achievement which obtained for her the wide reputation she enjoys. To those who are not, it may be interesting to know, that in the month of September last, herself and her father, at the imminent peril of their own lives, succeeded in rescuing a number of persons from the wreck of a steamboat, which foundered in Berwick Bay, on her passage from Hull to Dundee. The circumstances under which this exploit took place, were so remarkable, and indicated so generous a heroism in the old man, Darling, and his daughter, that the English people, always alive to personal bravery and merit, have heaped upon them both, the amplest honours. These, though from her sex and age the larger portion of them naturally fell to her share, Grace has borne, with a propriety that has greatly added to the favourable impression made by her courage, and her name is now on all lips as a theme of praise.

One of the engravings we prefix represents the wreck of the steamer, with the light-house, of which Grace's father was the keeper, and from which himself and his daughter, in a frail skiff, made their dangerous way to the distressed vessel, seen in the distance; and the other is a medallion portrait of these noble-minded persons, in which the likenesses are said to be faithfully preserved.

For the use of the engravings, we are indebted to our valued friend and correspondent, General Morris, of the New York Mirror.

As for M.S. in his remote Morpeth home – only twenty miles from Bamburgh, but more than 300 miles from London, he must have got immense pleasure from the publication of his report in *The Times*. I like to think of him, sitting by his peat fire with his bowl of porridge or drams of whisky, reading and rereading his own words, now immortalized for ever, destined to attract the notice of the great and the near-great throughout the realm.

For *The Times* was the one indispensable, authoritative source of information for England's rulers from the Palace down. In the 1830s there were over four hundred thriving provincial papers in the UK, but in the Grace Darling era *The Times* was the only consistently successful London daily paper; its circulation soared within a decade from 10,000 in 1830 to 18,500 by 1840 – huge, considering that the population of London was then about 1,600,000.

It was required reading for the growing middle class, the new-rich merchants – and the not-so-rich: the coffee houses furnished newspapers to be read on the spot for one penny by patrons, who for another penny could have a boiled egg. Coffee, including sugar and cream, was two pence. (As one advertisement put it, the coffee houses afforded 'advantages never before offered to the public, combining Economy, Health, Temperance and Instruction'.)

Queen Victoria disliked *The Times* and resented its growing influence. She proposed that 'the editor, the proprietor and the writers of such execrable publications should be ostracized from the circles of higher society'.[*]

Nevertheless it seems likely that the Queen, having first glanced through her own publicity as public figures are wont to do, noting that she had 'returned at a very slow pace and reached the Castle at 20 minutes past 4 o'clock', read on through the rest of the paper until she came to the heroic conduct of Miss Grace Horsley Darling.

Some weeks later Grace had a communication from the Treasury. While the idea may have originated from Queen Victoria's reading of M.S.'s thrilling account in *The Times* of 19 September, it is clear from its contents that the letter had to go a laborious route involving the concurrence of various high-ranking officials before it could be sent out:

---

[*]G. A. Cranfield, *The Press and Society*, Longman, 1978, p. 163.

Treasury Chambers
24 November 1838

Madam

The Lords Commissioners of Her Majesty's Treasury have commanded me to acquaint you that the attention of Her Majesty having been called to the circumstances attending the Wreck of the *Forfarshire* steamer in September last, on the Hawker Rock near Longstone Lighthouse, and to the intrepidity displayed by you, by which, under Divine Providence, the lives of nine persons were saved, in circumstances of great peril and difficulty, Her Majesty has signified Her Pleasure, that as a mark of Her Gracious approbation of your conduct on the occasion, the sum of Fifty Pounds should be paid to you; and Their Lordships have given direction to The Paymaster of Civil Services to make this payment to you accordingly,

I am,

Madam

Your obedient Servant

A. G. Speorman

P.S. You are at liberty to draw a Bill, according to the enclosed Form, upon the proper stamp for the amount.

Miss Grace Darling
Longstone Lighthouse

4. IN QUEST OF GRACE

In September 1985 Emma Tennant and I set out for Darling country, a two-hour drive from her house in Scotland. She had often visited the museum in Bamburgh: 'It's minuscule,' she said. 'About as big as an average sitting-room, and half that space is taken up by the actual coble in which Grace and her father rescued the crew. It's by no means a "frail skiff", as you'll see, but very stoutly built.'

Bamburgh (population 600), small and compact, reminds me of a child's toy village complete with fortified medieval castle, courtyards and battlements, perched atop a steep crag overlooking the streets and houses. Grace Darling memorials abound: her birthplace, later a post-office, and the house where she died, now a gift shop, each with its commemorative plaque. Close by is the museum, and across a tree-studded green the ancient parish church of St Aidan, dating from Norman times, where the Darlings were laid to rest.

Like the village, the museum is, as Emma had said, child-size, consisting of two rooms grandly designated in the museum brochure as 'West Room' and 'East Room'. A sign at the entrance advises that 'Visitors are requested to go round clockwise.' First we come to the coble on the side of which is painted in large white letters GRACE DAR-LING, clearly a latter-day embellishment. We marvel at its wonderfully solid construction – it had, in fact, been in service at the Longstone for many years before the Deed, and was subsequently given to William Brooks Darling, who used it thereafter for fishing.

On the opposite wall hangs a large framed chart: 'FARNE ISLAND WRECKS. For Those in Peril. John Harvey, 1976.' It is meticulously drawn to scale, depicting the coastline from Bamburgh to Seahouses, and beyond to the Farne Islands, coloured green for grass (very sparse),

blue for sea, brown for rocks. There are approximately seventeen islands in this treacherous reef, some mere rocks, submerged at high tide; a scene of desolation and tragedy, for next to each island on his chart Mr Harvey has

'Shipping on the Shore at Bamborough Castle' by John Varley, 1778–1842

(*over page*) Anonymous painting of Grace Darling – Grace Darling Museum, Bamburgh

recorded in fine script shipwrecks from the years 1462 to 1972, more than five hundred in all, and mostly with loss of life.

Leading the way clockwise through the second room,

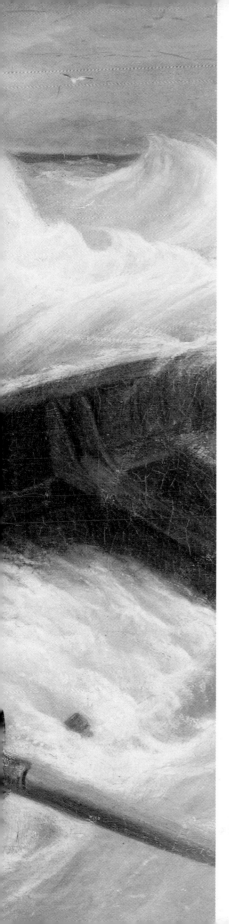

filled with Darling memorabilia, Emma is a first-rate guide – if she had a stick to point with she could pass for an Art Appreciation mistress conducting a tour of the Victoria and Albert Museum, or in America for a docent.

Here are the productions of the artists who journeyed to the Longstone in the wake of the wreck: portraits of Grace and her father; fanciful conceptions of the rescue; a charming lithograph of the Darling sitting-room showing Mrs Darling's spinning-wheel and a blazing fire at which survivors are warming their feet, soup being served all round. It's hard to form an idea of what Grace really looked like, as the portraits vary wildly from artist to artist, nose ranging from pert and short to austere Roman, hair from severely plain to romantically fluffy. The rescue pictures invariably show Grace with the streaming, windblown hair of legend (although we know from contemporary accounts that it was in curling rags at the time of the Deed). One of these, unsigned and undated, is instantly recognizable as the usual choice for reproduction in girls' magazines and annuals down the ages: Grace rowing alone in a frail skiff while between her and the lighthouse the seas like mountains rolled.

In a glass-enclosed case are displayed some twenty-five books in which Grace has been immortalized, the earliest – with far the prettiest binding – published within a year of the rescue, entitled *Grace Darling: The Maid of the Farnes*. Other cases contain locks of her hair, excerpts from Mr Darling's journal, fragments of the green and beige striped cotton frock that she wore to the rescue, each with Name of Donor appended. Apparently, as with the Beatles whose shirts were torn off their backs and ripped to pieces by screaming fans for treasured souvenirs, scraps of the Heroine's garment were in great demand throughout the realm.

Another cabinet features Grace's clothes: her christening robe, several dresses, shawls given to her by admirers, and – *pièce de résistance* – a bonnet of the finest black beaver lined with white satin, said in the local press to rival the 'famous Duchess of Sutherland bonnet'. (Never having heard of said famous bonnet I inquired at the V. & A.; alas, they too were unaware of its existence. Such is the ephemeral nature of fame in the bonnet department.) The letter accompanying the bonnet ran:

The rowing-boat, or 'coble', in which Grace and her father rescued the crew of the *Forfarshire* steamer, now housed at the Grace Darling Museum, and (below) exhibits at the Grace Darling Museum

Miss G. H. Darling, The Journeyman Hatters in the employ of Messrs. H. Hubback and Son, Berwick-on-Tweed, in consideration of your most praiseworthy conduct in rescuing (at the peril of your own life) a number of your fellow beings from a watery grave, request your acceptance of a Beaver which you will receive with this. Though but a trifle, yet it affords great pleasure to them to think that they shall in the least degree contribute to the protection of a Head which contains a Mind capable of braving the most fearful dangers in the cause of suffering humanity.

November 29th, 1838

Rounding the corner Emma leads me to a case of Grace Darling mementoes, mass-produced souvenirs and knick-knacks that attest to the entrepreneurial ingenuity of nineteenth-century manufacturers, alert even in those far-off days to the commercial value of a famous name: Grace Darling Cadbury chocolates, Grace Darling mugs, Grace Darling pen-wipers.

Hard by are relics salvaged from the *Forfarshire*, vast decorated china platters with scalloped edges, floral designs, a picture of the ship and something resembling a coat of arms ('Positively ducal,' said Emma, who should know), a gilt-scrolled tray, and some cutlery of Berlin silver.

Plate from the *Forfarshire* steamer – Grace Darling Museum

Interspersed amongst the main exhibits are gold and silver medals awarded to Grace and her father by various Humane Societies; a selection of her letters, written in a fine script; newspapers of the day recording the Deed. Amidst this reverential, near-sanctified collection, the museum committee who prepared and oversaw its contents allowed themselves one moment of levity: a framed picture postcard of a little boy and his dog, stranded at sea on their overturned boat, the boy shouting 'Haw! Grace Darling!'

There is much more: displays of poems about Grace by Wordsworth, Swinburne and many a lesser rhymester – some of whom, I thought, outdid those masters. For example, this, unsigned, from the *Berwick & Kelso Warder* of 17 November 1838:

With Grace's coble in the background, the RNLI donation box links the past to the present

ON MISS GRACE HORSLEY DARLING

Tho' *hoarsely* she has heard the flood
Contending with the wind,
With naught to cheer her solitude,
Nor to her race to bind
Yet she by nature seems endowed,
Though on a rock enshrined,
To be the *Grace* of womanhood,
And *Darling* of mankind.

The poet has cleverly worked in Grace's middle name,
Horsley, which was her mother's maiden name. Although
purists might object that one cannot *hear* things *hoarsely*
– and might point to other *non sequiturs* dragged in for the
sake of rhyming – the poem compares favourably with

Memorial of Grace Darling at
Bamburgh church

Wordsworth's appalling effort of a hundred lines, partly
because it is so much shorter.

Possibly due to watchful and solicitous editors, one will
search in vain through standard Wordsworth collections
for his tribute to Grace Darling.* The first several lines are
portent of what is to come:

Among the dwellers in the silent fields
The natural heart is touched, and public way
And crowded street resound with ballad strains,
Inspired by ONE whose very name bespeaks
Favour divine, exalting human love . . .

---

*It is, however, included under the heading 'Miscellaneous Poems',
in *The Poetical Works of William Wordsworth*, Oxford: Clarendon
Press.

Reading on, we get to 'A maiden gentle, yet, at duty's call/ Firm and unflinching . . .' and (we are still not half-way through) '"But courage, Father! Let us out to sea –/A few may yet be saved."' Comes the punchline:

Pious and pure, modest and yet so brave,
Though young so wise, though meek so resolute –
Might carry to the clouds and to the stars,
Yea, to celestial Choirs, GRACE DARLING'S name!

Emma and I are overwhelmed by the paradoxical immensity and scope of this very small collection, its encapsulation of every aspect of the legend – an experience akin to looking through a powerful microscope at a drop of water in which scores of surprising and mysterious objects, invisible to the naked eye, are revealed.

Having 'done' the museum we wander over to the church, another repository of much Darling lore. On one wall are three memorial stained-glass windows of remarkable hideousness depicting Faith, Fortitude and Charity, the central figure bearing an oar. In the transept is a full-length statue of Grace recumbent, an oar at her side, replica of the one in the churchyard mausoleum.

In the churchyard are the Darling family graves with headstones recording their births and deaths, and Grace's mausoleum, which in its dramatic setting on a promontory overlooking the sea assumes the aspect of a mini Taj Mahal. The original, erected shortly after her death, disintegrated because the wrong sort of stone was used. Another, of different and (to my mind) inferior design, was put up in 1885.

Our next stop is the nearby village of Seahouses (known in Grace's day as North Sunderland), where we call on Emma's friend Peter Hawkey, a naturalist employed by the National Trust. For several months each year Mr Hawkey and five or six colleagues live on Brownsman Island, now a wildlife sanctuary, in the very cottage where Grace spent the first ten years of her life. Born in Bamburgh, she was transported to Brownsman at the age of three weeks, her father being at the time assistant light-keeper to his own father, Robert Darling. Brownsman lighthouse was considered inadequate for its purpose, badly placed to guide vessels at sea beyond the Outer

Brownsman, the old lighthouse,
Farne Islands

Farnes. In 1825 Trinity House* decreed the building of a
new lighthouse on Longstone, the outermost island of the
Farnes group, a desolate rock where not even a blade of
grass could grow.

Judging by Mr Hawkey's description, Brownsman must
have been paradise compared to Longstone. There was a
pond to attract fowl and walled gardens in which one
could keep livestock and grow flowers and vegetables.

*Trinity House: a guild established in Henry VII's reign. Controls
and supervises lighthouses on English coasts.

After the move the Darlings continued to tend their gardens on Brownsman, a two-mile row from Longstone. And how are the earwigs faring today? I asked. Still very numerous, said Mr Hawkey.

William Darling, himself a keen amateur naturalist who corresponded with ornithologists on the mainland and contributed specimens to natural-history museums, was the first to keep accurate records of domestic and migrant birds.

There have been few improvements on Brownsman since the Darling era. 'It's very much in the same state, except that now we have bottled gas – still no electricity – and an indoor netty earth closet.' But the weather has changed for the better over the years, he said. 'In those days the storms must have been incredibly severe, to the point where the sea swept into the ground floor of the cottage, and sometimes the pond froze over. This never happens now.'

I asked about the hazards of the Darling rescue mission – how great was the danger to Grace and Mr Darling? 'Well, no doubt they did a very brave thing. But Mr Darling was an experienced seaman. He waited until low tide, and took the safest route, in the lee of the rocks. I shouldn't think their lives were in much danger.'

By now, I thought I had the picture fairly well in focus. But no. 'Tomorrow, Aunt Decca,' said Emma firmly, 'I've booked us to go out to the Longstone Lighthouse on a tour boat. It's only a three-hour trip.' It was, she added, an open boat: 'Better put on several good stout jerseys, gumboots and a mac. It's likely to be pouring, usually is up this way.'

In vain I pleaded – 'But why don't *you* go, and describe it all to me when you get back. That way I can write it up and pretend I'd gone, nobody will ever know . . .' Absolutely not, said she, getting quite stern. As a researcher, surely I should know that an eyewitness account is *de rigueur*? Properly admonished, I acceded; and, as Emma had predicted, was very glad I had done so.

Surprisingly – for this was mid-September, long past the normal tourist season – the boat was crowded to capacity, every inch of the wooden seating along the sides taken. At least fifty passengers, ranging from early middle age to very old, some even on crutches, had paid their £3 for this dubious treat. So we are off to the Farne Islands.

The boatman keeps up a running commentary in broad

Northumbrian. Of principal interest are Brownsman Island, as a National Trust bird sanctuary out of bounds for trippers, and Longstone, home of that braw lassie Grace Darling. I repeated to him what Peter Hawkey had told us about the relatively safe route taken by the Darlings, to which he replied 'But still, it was pretty steep for a lady. She did vurrah well.'

The huge bird colonies on Brownsman, which we pass within hailing distance, are an awesome sight, great armies of birds etched against the sky standing guard on the high rocks, a profusion of nests lower down. The boatman points out the different species, tern, cormorant, puffin – no wonder Mr Darling took such an avid interest, and was a lifetime observer of these.

We disembark on Longstone, the aged and those on crutches given an able assist by younger and spryer types. There is a rough path from our landing place to the lighthouse – but as Peter Hawkey had cautioned, 'one has to mind one's step every inch of the way. You can't look up – which is rather a pity, the sky's so beautiful in these parts.'

As for the lighthouse itself, it is not a thing of beauty – it's just a very nice, very serviceable structure for its purpose and extremely durable. Gazing up at this large edifice, it occurs to me that a London friend has been living in a state of frustration for many months, her flat all a-jumble while she tries to get an extra room built on. I compose a letter to her in my head: 'Now, if you were only building a lighthouse on the furthermost isle of the Farnes, a barren and desolate rock off the stormy coast of Northumberland, in 1825 when there were no trains or steamers, just horse-drawn wagons and row boats, and you had to transport the stones from a quarry in Yorkshire to build an eighty-five-foot tower to include ample living space for a family of eleven plus occasional guests and, of course, a working lantern – you'd have the whole thing finished in less than a year.'

In fact it took about ten months, as recorded in Mr Darling's *Journal*, beginning in March 1825 with a visit to Brownsman of the surveying engineer, who arrived with other dignitaries in the Trinity yacht. In April, a barracks was built on Longstone to house the workmen – the same rough-hewn stone building that thirteen years later provided shelter for the *Forfarshire* survivors. (In 1844 the

Sandwich terns in flight by Longstone Lighthouse, Farne Islands

barracks was demolished by a violent gale, and has since
been replaced by outbuildings to accommodate today's
lightkeepers, men who no longer live on the island with
their families but work in revolving shifts of two weeks at
a time.)

    Mr J. Nelson, architect, and Thomas Wade, foreman,
stayed with the Darlings on Brownsman for much of the
time. In September, the Duke of Northumberland came to
see the new tower on Longstone. By 17 December, 'the
principal part of the workmen paid off', the lantern was
erected. In February 1826: 'Longstone light first lighted
and Brownsman light extinguished.'

    The interior of the lighthouse was perfectly designed to
make a comfortable home for the large Darling family.

Longstone Lighthouse today

The ground floor is one big, all-purpose living-room, similar in its plan to the newly gentrified workers' dwellings in Fulham and Kentish Town in which walls dividing sitting-room, dining-room and kitchen have been knocked down to make for more space. From the living-room a spiral staircase winds up to three circular bedroom floors, thence to the lantern at the top. Here the Darlings took turns keeping watch through the night; and here Mr Darling conducted a one-room school, instructing his children in the scriptures, geography, natural history and certain approved poets such as Milton and Robert Burns.

Today, one cannot go into the erstwhile living-room. Its capacious wood stove, Mrs Darling's spinning-wheel, the furniture made by one of the older boys who was apprenticed to a joiner, have long since been replaced by the machinery that now assures the functioning of the light. The boys' bedroom on the first floor, once lined with bunk beds, and the second floor bedrooms are also filled with machinery and supplies. Only Grace's small, monastic bedroom on the third floor remains inviolate, a sacrosanct memorial to her name and fame.

We scramble – or are lugged, depending on age and condition – back into the tour boat for the final adventure: retracing the rescue route. Contrary to Emma's predictions, the weather is balmy, the sea flat calm. But as we approach the Big Harcar there is a noticeable swell, and quite a bit of dashing spray splashes over us tourists, evoking many a giggle and 'Mind that wave, Ernie!' from the passengers.

I strained my eyes – wishing, actually, for second sight and a glimpse of the shades of those long-ago rescued and rescuers. How to reconstruct that terrifying scene – Mr Darling leaping from the coble to the rock, Grace plying the oars while he sorted out the quick from the dead and decided who to take back on that first perilous journey to the lighthouse? None of them appeared except in my imagination. But I have to agree with our boatman: 'It was pretty steep for a lady. She did very well.'

5. PURE AS THE AIR AROUND HER

The best account of Grace's life on the Longstone is her own, written in answer to one of her admirers who had bombarded her with inquiries about her childhood and had made the fatuous comment that 'We fancy you so used to the waves that you have pleasure riding out in a rough sea.' To this Grace replied with evident exasperation, 'You requested me to let you know whether I felt pleasure to be out in a rough sea, which I can assure you there is none, I think, to any person in their sober senses.'

She goes on to describe her education and upbringing, which seem made to order for the inculcation of those virtues and moral outlook that would endear the future heroine to her nineteenth-century contemporaries:

I have been brought up on the Islands, learned to read and write by my parents, and knit, spin, and soe, or sew; indeed I have no time to spare, but when I have been on the Main I am quite surprised to see people generally after what they call getting their day's work done, they sit down, some to play at cards, which I do not understand, perhaps as well, for my father says they are some of the Devil's books; others to read romances, novels and plays, which are books my father will not allow a place in our house, for he says they are throwing away time. Our books are principally Divinity; the authors, Bishop Wilson, Willison, Boston, Milton, Hervey, Bunyan, Ambrose, Newton, Marshall, Cowper, Flavel, Baxter and others, with a good many of the Religious Tract Society's Publications; and Geography, History, Voyages and Travels, with Maps, so that Father can show us any part of the World, and give us a description of the people, manners and customs, so it is our own blame if we be ignorant of either what is done, or what ought to be done.

The same dim-witted correspondent asked in her effusive way, 'Does time never pass heavily when confined for weeks together to the same spot?' Grace's sharp rejoinder:

I have seven apartments in the house to keep in a state fit to be inspected every day by Gentlemen, so that my hands are kept very busy that I never think the time long, but often too short. I have often had occasion to be in the boat with my Father for want of better help, but never at the saving of any lives before, and I pray God may never be again. . . You will perhaps be aware that our duty as Light-keepers requires one person to be in attendance at this season almost every hour out of the 24, Sunday to Saturday.

This letter, along with many others written by Grace and Mr Darling, is quoted in *Grace Darling: Her True Story. From Unpublished Papers in Possession of Her Family.* This excellent seventy-five-page booklet, published in 1880, more than forty years after the wreck of the *Forfarshire*, was compiled by Grace's eldest sister Thomasin,* a seamstress who lived in Bamburgh, with the help of a local writer, Daniel Atkinson.

Her True Story is Thomasin Darling's attempt to set the record straight on a number of counts in which, she says, 'accuracy has suffered' due to the 'glowing language, aided by imagination' of innumerable chroniclers of the wreck and rescue. For example, she points out that it would have been impossible for Grace to have heard the cries of the shipwrecked crew, fully half a mile distant in a direct line, in the midst of a northern gale which would have carried any sound in the opposite direction. Thomasin would have hated the lyrics of the 'Grace Darling Song', according to which 'Her father cried "'Tis madness/To face that raging sea"', and '"Return, or doomed are we!"' Of Mr Darling, she writes:

---

*The family nomenclature is slightly confusing as the same names recur. To sort it out:

    William Darling (born 1786) married
    Thomasin Horsley (born 1774) in the year 1805.
Their children, in order of birth:
    William (born 1806)
    Thomasin ⎫
    Mary Ann ⎭ (twins, born 1807)
    Job Horsley (born 1810)
    Elizabeth Grace (born 1811)
    Robert (born 1814)
    Grace Horsley (born 1815, the year of Waterloo)
    George Alexander ⎫
    William Brooks ⎭ (twins, born 1817)

. . . the romanticists who, in the affair of the Forfarshire, made the entreaties of his daughter overrule his judgment, did not know about whom they wrote. It is very likely that the proposal to aid her father in the boat first came from Grace; but had he not himself thought the attempt practicable, he was not the man to endanger her life and his own in weak concession to girlish importunity. His own account, – 'We agreed that if we could get to them some of them would be able to assist us back,' is doubtless a plain statement of the simple truth.

But Thomasin Darling's praiseworthy effort to sort fact from fiction was, as it turned out, too little and too late. Sales of *True Story* must have been limited to a few local people, judging by a letter from Miss Darling to her collaborator:

Our book, I believe, is selling pretty well, had two parties called yesterday, told them where they would get it, I have no doubt of them as they intend calling again for me to write my name in them.

The arduous routine of normal lighthouse drudgery as described in Grace's letter was dramatically disrupted shortly after the rescue. The post-Deed transformation of life on the Longstone – the invasion of reporters, artists, sightseers, the unending stream of presents to be acknowledged and letters to be answered – became a dreadful burden to the Darlings *père et fille*. What Mrs Darling thought about it all is not known: she remains a shadowy figure, constantly at her spinning-wheel. Twelve years older than her husband, she was in her late sixties at the time, and although she helped to launch the coble there would have been no question of her going out to the wreck. According to *Her True Story*, Mrs Darling swooned from anxiety when her husband and daughter rowed out in the storm, but recovered to help attend to the injured when they got back; however, nobody thought to ask her opinion of the event.

Among the first on the scene were the artists, agog for what in America the White House press agents call 'photo opportunities'. There were as yet no cameras in England, hence no swarms of shutterbugs snapping away; but their predecessors, the artist or sculptor whose product could be mass-produced via mezzotint, lithograph or casts of busts must have been every bit as importunate, demanding and

June 31ˢᵗ 1846   M Laidler

Thomasin Darling
Late Longstone Light June 31ˢᵗ 1846

The Mother of Grace Darling

irksome to the Darling family as their latter-day counter-parts, the television crews and colour-supplement photographers.

At least twelve artists are known to have gone out to the Longstone, and many of these were advertising their wares within days of their visit. Thus David Dunbar, a sculptor whose bust of Grace is now in the National Portrait Gallery, took an advertisement in the *Berwick & Kelso Warder* of 27 October 1838:

Bust of Grace Darling
by D. Dunbar

BUSTS OF GRACE DARLING AND HER FATHER
Mr. Dunbar most respectfully intimates
that he has during the present month,
modelled Busts of the above Humane
Individuals at their residence.

He adds that the busts can be seen at his rooms in
Newcastle, and that finished casts can be had for one
guinea each.

For the painters, no less than for the lowly penny-a-
liners, the Darling story must have presented an irresist-
ible twofold lure: the inherent drama of the wreck and
rescue, a subject to give fullest rein to the creative
imagination, and the prospect of a quick cash turnover
through sales of the product to an eagerly receptive public.
For example, Henry Perlee Parker, one of three Darling
portraitists to merit a mention in the *Dictionary of
National Biography* (the others are Thomas Musgrave Joy
and James Wilson Carmichael, all exhibitors in the Royal
Academy), excelled in paintings of smugglers, according
to the *DNB*, and was known by the sobriquet 'Smuggler
Parker': 'His pictures were remarkable for their selling
powers, a fact largely due to a fortunate choice of subject.'

Fortunate for Mr Parker, perhaps, but less so for the
beleaguered objects of artistic endeavour. On 17 October,
less than six weeks after the wreck, Mr Darling issued a
cry of distress, an SOS to the newspapers written in draft
on the back of an application for 'a few sittings':

Dear Sir,
Please to acquaint the Public in your paper that within the
last twelve days I and my Daughter have sat to no less than
seven portrait painters, amongst which is Mr. Andrews from
Edinburgh, Mr. Laidler [*sic* – it was a Miss Laidler] from Shields,
Mr. Watson from Newcastle, Mr. E. Hastings from Durham, a
first-rate portrait painter, with three other gentlemen who did
not leave their names. In this place it is attended with a great
deal of inconvenience; it would require me to have nothing else
to do; therefore hopes the Public will be satisfied, as they can
have correct likenesses from any of the above named.
                    Your most humble Servant,
                         Wm. Darling
I have had three letters today making application for sittings.*

Her True Story, 19 October 1838.

Of the artists named in Mr Darling's letter, Mr Edward Hastings of Durham proved to be, if not much of a painter, a gifted and assiduous entrepreneur. His portrait of Grace, simpering prettily in a beribboned bonnet and elegant shawl, may be an artistic disaster but was an enduring commercial success; the prints sold in quantity from Scotland to London, and eventually were reproduced as frontispieces in at least two biographies.

Aside from straight advertising, successful sales strategy depended on the planted news item such as this, from the *Durham Chronicle* of 23 November 1838:

[Hastings's] head of old Darling is a fine phrenological study. . . Grace Darling's countenance is of an exceedingly pleasing cast . . . Mrs. Darling appears to be a homely old matron, of a kindly disposition. . . The portraits are admirably painted, and as works of art, independently of all connection with the fearful tale that has given to the family an interest in every heart, have a strong claim to public favour.

And this from *The Times* of 17 November 1838, quoting the *Edinburgh Observer*:

Mr Hastings, an artist, of Durham, shortly after the wreck of the Forfarshire steamer, visited the Fern Islands and took the portraits of the Darling family. A finer head than that of William Darling we have rarely seen and there is a quiet look of steady determination and serious thought in the well-formed countenance of Grace Darling, which clearly denotes her undaunted character.

Mr Hastings, equally undaunted, had a brilliant scheme for jacking up sales. The following summer, just ahead of the tourist season, he wrote to Mr Darling. In his letter dated 1 July 1839, he lamented his difficulties with the lithographic engravers, whose charges were far higher than he had expected – his expenses, he said, had mounted to above £45. So he proposed to send a number of prints to the Lighthouse

in hopes that as you are very likely to be visited by many a boat-load this summer many of these might be sold and we will divide the profits whatever they may bring either at the Islands or on shore. I do not think you must put above 2s. or at the most 2s. 6d. each upon them but judge for yourself when you have an opportunity of trying them.

Photograph
of William Darling
in later life

Whether or not Mr Darling fell in with this profit-sharing plan is not known. In any event, by the summer of 1839 he and Grace were awash in cash.

Money and presents poured in from individual well-wishers, or raised by subscription through the newspapers, or by contributions collected at civic meetings throughout the realm. These gatherings were mostly convened for the purpose of presenting petitions to the Queen and Parliament urgently demanding mandatory inspection of steamships, to forestall any repetition of the *Forfarshire* disaster. There was an invariable rider to the main order of business, as reported in this news item, from the *Sun* of 29 September 1838, of a meeting called by the mayor of Newcastle, T. Headlam. The meeting having voted unanimously for government regulation of steamships, Mr J. Brandling proposed to raise a subscription for the Darlings:

He had much pleasure in advocating this cause, because there was a female connected with it, and he was always ready to assist them by every means in his power. [One can visualize broad winks at that sly rogue Brandling.] If ever there was a woman that well deserved the thanks of her country, it was the daughter of Darling. He did not like to raise any thing like jealousy, but no doubt they formerly called themselves lords of the creation, and they must now allow a female character to be no way inferior, for that woman exhibited a firmness of mind, a duty to her father, and duty as a Christian, equal to any man in the country.

Aside from money, medals from Humane Societies, requests for Grace's signature, and presents of books, sewing boxes and the like arrived in profusion, the main conduit being the ever-solicitous Mr Smeddle of the Crewe Trust in Bamburgh, who would row over to the Longstone loaded with letters and gifts. Grace, hard pressed, wrote to one friend:

According to your request you will receive a few signatures, but you must not promise them too many, for I am both 'deed swere and unco ill o'.' Perhaps you would scarcely believe it, I have signed about 110 cards for Mr. Smeddle alone, and I don't know how many to others.

This sorry state of affairs did not improve as weeks, then months, then years went by. In 1840, two years after the wreck, William Howitt (1792–1879), a prolific and popular travel writer, visited the Darlings and described the scene in his book *Visits to Remarkable Places* (1842):

... the foolish, though natural avidity of the mob of wonder-lovers, who in steam boat loads have flocked thither, filling that tall lighthouse several stories high, till nobody could stir. . . the house is literally crammed with presents of one kind or another, including a considerable number of books. . .

Grace, he wrote, 'shuns public notice, and is even troubled at the visits of the curious'. His description of her is far more satisfactory in conjuring up what she actually looked like than are the wildly different portraits of those dreaming, scheming artists:

She is not like any of the portraits of her. She is a little simple, modest young woman, I should say five or six and twenty. She is neither tall nor handsome; but she has the most gentle, quiet, amiable look, and the sweetest smile that I ever saw in a person of her station and appearance. . . Her figure is by no means striking; quite the contrary; but her face is full of sense, modesty, and genuine goodness; and that is just the character she bears.

Earlier scribes, newspaper reporters who had dashed out to the Longstone immediately after word of Grace's heroic Deed became known on the mainland, had much the same to say about her appearance. The *Berwick & Kelso Warder* of 22 September 1838 said, 'Grace is nothing masculine in her appearance, although she has so stout a heart. In person she is about the middle size, of a comely countenance – rather fair for an islander – and with an expression of benevolence and softness most truly feminine in every point of view.'

'Our Own Correspondent' of the *Shipping & Mercantile Gazette* (20 September 1838) reported that

many have been to see this heroine, and all have been agreeably disappointed in her appearance. She is not the amazon that many would suppose her to be, but as modest and unassuming a young woman as you can imagine. She is not more than five feet three or four inches in height, her figure is rather slight than otherwise, and her features, though not what can be called absolutely pretty, are regular, and their expression is remarkably pleasing.

A curious by-product of fame in Grace's day was the yearning of admirers for bits of the famous one's hair. Whether Freud or his successors, pioneers in the study of peculiar and arcane fetishes, ever addressed themselves to this quirky wish for hirsute souvenirs of public figures I do not know; nor do I intend to find out, as the subject is beyond the scope of this book.

Contemporary newspapers made caustic comments on the phenomenon, as in this example (one of many) in *The Times* of 25 October 1838, quoting from the *Durham Advertiser*:

GRACE DARLING.— This humane and heroic female received a letter a few days ago from a lady at Alnwick, enclosing a £5 note, and requesting in return for it a lock of her hair. Several ladies who have recently visited the Fern Islands have solicited and obtained similar tokens of remembrance and there seems a probability, if the demand should continue, that she will, ere long, have to seek an artificial, in exchange for the natural, covering of her head – unless indeed by the use of Bears' Grease or Macassor Oil she should succeed in producing a regular succession of crops. It appears somewhat absurd to endeavour thus to deprive Miss Darling of her ringlets . . .

The many locks displayed in the Bamburgh museum, each meticulously tagged with the donor's name, are of a remarkable range of shades from golden to dark brown to rich mouse – as one visitor noted, 'Her hair seems to have been the colour of a Cheshire cat's.' A possible explanation is suggested by Grace's biographer, Constance Smedley, who writes that quantities of hair purported to be authentic samples of the heroine's tresses were exhibited in shop windows, and offered publicly for sale:

Her brother, George Alexander, when having a shave in a barber's in Newcastle, was asked to buy a lock by a vendor who was hawking a trayful from place to place. 'What did he do?' his daughter was asked. 'Kicked the man out o' the shop. It was no hair o' Gracie's,' was the reply.

For the coastal fishermen of Northumberland and their

families, whose livelihood depended on daily exposure to the awesome terrors of potentially lethal seas, the nation-wide adulation of Grace – who had, after all, merely taken an oar as anyone would, on a one-way trip to the wreck – became a cause of resentment, exacerbated as years went by.

In *Her True Story*, Thomasin Darling blames the 'inflated descriptions by the pen, or exaggerated illustrations by the pencil, which attribute to Grace Darling and her father impossible achievements'. She cites a particularly annoying and erroneous article in the *Illustrated London News* of 10 June 1865, written shortly after Mr Darling's death (and twenty-seven years after the wreck of the *Forfarshire*.) She quotes the following passage:

For it must always be remembered that when Grace Darling had in vain implored the assembled boatmen of the shore to make one effort to rescue the drowning people from the wreck, her father was moved by the girl's tears of pity and disappointment. He exclaimed 'the wench shall hae her wull,' and launching his own boat, with her alone to help him at the oar, went forth. . .

Thomasin's comment on this:

The fiction is here manifest, for there were not any boatmen at the Longstone to be implored. 'The assembled boatmen' were at North Sunderland, six or seven miles off; and the particular phraseology attributed to William Darling is as much the author's as the rest of the story.

Decades earlier, William Howitt had detected much the same resentment in his conversations with the 'common people' of the district *en route* to his visit to the Longstone in 1840:

The most characteristic thing is, that all the common people about, and particularly the sailors and fishermen, deny her all merit. The first person that I asked about her was a young girl of about sixteen years of age, who was going along towards Bamburgh as I approached it. 'Well, do you know Grace Darling?' 'O, ay, varry weel.' 'I suppose she is much thought of hereabouts?' 'Much thought of! Nooa, Grace Darling is thought nothing particular, only except by those a good way off.' 'But that was a brave action of hers?' 'O, nooa, there was no danger. It was at low-water; and the sea was quite smooth; anybody could have done what she did.'

The harbour-master of North Sunderland, to whom Mr Howitt applied for a boat to the Longstone, was of the same opinion:

'What, is it Grace Darling that you want to see?' 'Yes.' 'Phoh! It's all humbug. It was that painter chap that made all the noise about her; he knew what he was about. It was a good speculation for him. They pretend to say that Grace and her father saved the nine people from the wreck; they did nothing of the sort; the people saved themselves. They walked across from the vessel at low water to the next island and the Darlings fetched them off when the water was smooth. . .'

Mr Howitt ascribes these views to envy of Grace for the money and honour she had won for her daring deed. Conversely, higher in the social scale he found nothing but admiration:

The well-informed gentry say that it was a most noble action . . . indeed all the gentry with whom I had an opportunity of speaking on that part of the coast, had but one voice in honour of Grace Darling's courage and generous devotion; as well as of her general prudence and admirable character.

6. THE CLASSES AND THE MASSES

The comings and goings of reporters, painters, poets and sightseers who visited Longstone in the wake of the Deed did not, it seems, do much to widen Grace's limited horizon, or even to alert her to the existence of a world beyond the Farne Islands and their immediate vicinity. Judging by her letters, she was a fairly intelligent girl with a certain sharpness of wit, yet strangely incurious. If she had had half an eye open, or half an ear cocked, to events of the day she might have observed that history was being made almost within hailing distance of her home ground.

Now for a breath – or a lungful – of foetid air, possibly a welcome relief from all that pure air around the Longstone lighthouse and the unswerving rectitude, devotion to Duty and unquestioning obedience to authority of its inhabitants.

During the 1830s and 1840s, years that spanned Grace's childhood, her sudden fame and her early death, England was in the grip of a deep, almost uninterrupted economic depression that engulfed much of the nascent industrial working-class and spread throughout the agricultural districts, thus affecting labourers in all categories. In Parliament, reformers campaigned for the Ten Hours Bill (including a provision that children between eight and thirteen should be restricted to six and a half hours of work per day), and against the Poor Law which required that the destitute be locked up in workhouses, there to live and labour in conditions of virtual slavery, in order to qualify for any form of relief.

The major literary event of 1838 (year of the Deed) was the publication of *Oliver Twist*, intended by its author to wring hearts and stir consciences to a recognition of the frightful plight of England's growing population of paupers. But as it would have fallen squarely into the category of 'romances, novels and plays, which are books my father will not allow a place in our house, for he says they are throwing away time', Grace would not have been exposed to its powerful message.

Easily the most spectacular protest against intolerable conditions was that of the short-lived Chartist movement, which flourished from 1835 to about 1848.* Throughout those years Chartists harried the hated aristocracy and the despised 'shopocracy' – as they called the newly ascendant middle classes – with gigantic meetings to which workers flocked by the tens of thousands, seditious and inflammatory speeches, and insurrectionary marches in the major towns from London to the north of England.

Two leaflets of the era from Newcastle, preserved in the Tyne and Wear archives, give some indication of the intensity of the struggle.

The first thunders out the message in a headline of solid black letters an inch high:

GENERAL STRIKE!

The strike, agreed upon by delegates 'from above Forty Surrounding Districts', was set for 12 August 1839. An enumeration of some major grievances follows:

MEN OF THE NORTH OF ENGLAND!
We submit to you a Sample of the Wrongs that have been done you, and we trust to your own Spirit and Energy for finding Means to bring these Wrongs and Oppressions speedily to an End.

Within the last Seventy Years the Aristocracy robbed the People of Eight Millions of Acres of Common Lands Apportioned to them for an Inheritance by England's one good King, the immortal Alfred.

In a Space of Thirty Years, from 1776 till 1815, the Boroughmongers borrowed Eight Hundred Millions Sterling for the Purpose of Murdering the Patriots of America and France. Not the Estates of the Aristocracy, but you, Working Men, and your Children are Mortgaged for ever to pay this unjust Debt.

---

*Their principal demand was universal male suffrage, the right to vote then being restricted to property owners. Female suffrage was not at that time even an issue.

GENERAL STRIKE!

AT a Weekly Meeting of the Council of the Northern Political Union, held on Wednesday Evening, August 7, *1839* Letters were read and Reports given in from above Forty of the surrounding Districts, all of which were unanimous for a total and general Strike from Labour on MONDAY, the 12th of August.

The following Resolution was then moved, seconded, and carried, with only one Dissentient :—

" That in accordance with the Wish so universally expressed the Council of the Northern Political Union approve of the Strike taking place on Monday, the Day above named.

MEN OF THE NORTH OF ENGLAND!

We submit to you a Sample of the Wrongs that have been done you, and we trust to your own Spirit and Energy for finding Means to bring those Wrongs and Oppressions speedily to an End.

Within the last Seventy Years the Aristocracy robbed the People of Eight Millions of Acres of Common Lands. Apportioned to them for an Inheritance by England's one good King, the immortal Alfred.

In a Space of Thirty Years, from 1776 till 1815, the Boroughmongers borrowed Eight Hundred Millions Sterling for the Purpose of Murdering the Patriots of America and France. Not the Estates of the Aristocracy, but you, Working Men, and your Children are Mortgaged for ever to pay this unjust Debt.

In 1819 this enormous Debt—contracted in a depreciated Paper Currency—was made payable in Gold, adding thereby a full Third to the Wealth of the Jew Fundholder, to be wrung from the Misery, and Tears, and Hunger of the People.

The Property Tax, amounting to Seventeen Millions annually, was repealed at the Close of the French War, and the whole Burthen thrown on the Shoulders of the People.

Not content with this mighty Injustice the Landlords established the present Corn Laws to famish you, your Wives, and Children, in order to double their enormous Rent Rolls.

This brings us up to the Passing of the Reform Bill ; that Measure, we fondly hoped, would remove our Grievances. For seven Years we reposed with Confidence on the Justice and Patriotism of the Middle Classes. Let us examine the FRUITS which the Reform Bill brought forth ! " By their fruits ye shall know them."

First—The despotic and bloody Irish Coercion Bill, which gave to Military Officers the Power to transport or hang the Irish People without either Judge or Jury.

Second—The hideous and accurst New Poor Law, which tears assunder the dearest and the holiest Ties of the human Heart, which consigns even the Old and Infirm to FAMISH amid the Gloom and SOLITUDE of a Dungeon Workhouse.

Third—The open Violation of the Constitution of Canada, and the inhuman Murder of the gallant Hearts which stood forth to defend their Rights—Rights given and guaranteed to them by our own Government.

Englishmen ! you saw these crying-to-Heaven-iniquities— you saw that there was no redress to be expected from the perfumed Lord-lings and Money-mongers who usurp the Legislation of the Country—you petitioned these Creatures—you demanded that they should make way for honester Men—your Petition, though signed by Twelve Hundred Thousand Men, has been rejected with as much Con-tempt as if you were mere Children, and those Honourables were Pedagogues able and willing to whip you into Submission.

Englishmen ! you asked for a Redress of Grievances, and your answer is a Bourbon Police—you asked for the Rights of Citizens, you are answered by fresh Outrage and unexampled Wrong—you ask a fair Day's Wages for a fair Day's Work, you are answered by Five Thousand additional Bayonets—and your best and your bravest are hurled into the Dungeons of Gloom.

Is there a Working Man in England so degraded as to slavishly submit to these Wrongs and Insults ?—Let him submit—let Disgrace follow, and Remorse haunt his coward Soul to the latest Hour of his Existence ; but let all that is virtuous, all that is good, all that has a Drop of British Blood in their Veins stand forward and vindicate that Freedom which never yet was made the Spoil of either Foreign Foe or Domestic Tyrant.

Men of the North of England ! be not baffled or deluded by the insolent Pretentions of Men who tell you that it is illegal to strike Work—your Labour is your own—you can do with it what you please—you are not yet sunk below the Level of the West Indian Slave.

We approve of the General Strike because it seems to be the only peaceable way in which the Power of the People can be made felt by the bad Men who oppress them. We hope to see ourselves, our Country, and Posterity rescued from Slavery without the shedding of one Drop of human Blood—we trust that the Lesson now about to be taught to the idle and impudent Consumers will have the speedy Effect of admitting those Men into the Constitution, without whom the Waters of England would be without a Ship and her Lands would be a solitary and noiseless Desert.

BY ORDER OF THE COUNCIL OF THE NORTHERN POLITICAL UNION.

SOLD FOR ONE HALFPENNY.

NEWCASTLE UPON-TYNE : PRINTED BY JOHN BELL, SIDE. *8 August 1839*

THE
MAYOR
AND
MAGISTRATES
OF THE
BOROUGH
OF
Newcastle upon Tyne,

Hereby assure the *well-disposed* of the **WORKING CLASSES**, that they will be carefully protected against the *Violence* of any who may endeavour to deter them, by *Intimidation* or otherwise, from following their Occupations; and that Persons attempting to intimidate will be punished with the utmost Rigour.---The Inhabitants are urgently enjoined to avoid Street Crowds.

JOHN FIFE, Mayor.

Police Office, Aug. 12, 1839.

Wm. Heaton, Printer, Newcastle.

The leaflet continues in this vein, castigating the landlords who 'established the present Corn Laws to famish
you, your Wives and Children'; the 'despotic and bloody
Irish Coercion Bill, which gave to Military Officers the
Power to transport or hang the Irish People without either
Judge or Jury'; 'the hideous and accurst New Poor Law . . .'
and winds up,

Men of the North of England! Be not baffled or deluded by the
insolent Pretentions of Men who tell you that it is illegal to
strike Work – your Labour is your own – you can do with it what
you please – you are not yet sunk below the Level of the West
Indian Slave. We approve of the General Strike because it seems
to be the only peaceable way in which the Power of the People
can be made felt by the bad Men who oppress them. . .

The bad men were not slow to respond. The second leaflet,
signed by John Fife, mayor, and issued by the Police Office
on 12 August 1839 – date of the scheduled strike –
proclaims in equally large letters:

THE
MAYOR
AND
MAGISTRATES
OF THE
BOROUGH
OF
Newcastle upon Tyne

Hereby assure the *well-disposed* of the
WORKING CLASSES, that they will be
carefully protected against the *Violence* of
any who may endeavour to deter them, by
their Occupations; and that Persons
attempting to intimidate will be punished
with the utmost Rigour. The Inhabitants
are urgently enjoined to avoid Street
Crowds.

M. A. Richardson, whose vivid prose we have already
sampled in his account of Grace Darling's perilous exertions and noble achievement, devotes twenty pages of his

Local Historian's Table Book to the activities of the Chartists, their allies, their enemies. Published in 1842, only three years after the call for a general strike, Richardson's report conveys a sense of immediacy not found in most history books.

'With the turn of the year [1839],' he writes, 'did the Charter strike deep roots. Meetings were held without number, in all the towns, villages and hamlets of the county of Durham and on the coast of Northumberland. By the month of March, the whole of the district above mentioned was in a perfect ferment...'

The shopocracy fought back: '... the magistrates of the district set to work right earnestly in the appointing of special constables' augmented by an armed troop of the 7th Dragoons. 'Monster meetings' held throughout the spring and summer of 1839 were followed by street riots, scenes of 'violent outbreak and destruction of property to a considerable amount, and nearly too of life'. Chartist leaders were rounded up and arrested on charges such as 'holding a seditious meeting', committing a riot, etc.

Nobody, it seems, was actually killed during the uprisings, which consisted mainly of large crowds 'yelling and roaring with such uproarious violence as to rouse and terrify the sleeping inhabitants ... The respectable inhabitants of these streets were, as will naturally be imagined, dreadfully alarmed, for the triumphant yells set up after each successive act of demolition, were truly appalling.'

All this was going on in Newcastle, northern stronghold of the Chartists. During the same spring and summer Grace, a mere fifty miles away, would be painstakingly at work writing her thank-you letters, snipping bits of hair to enclose if asked for, and supplying dozens of autographs for Mr Smeddle, plus soldiering on at her regular task of polishing up the seven lighthouse apartments so they would be 'fit to be inspected every day by Gentlemen'.

It is unlikely that Grace ever heard of the Chartist movement; even if she had, she would not have been remotely sympathetic to its goals. (One can safely assume that Bamburgh and North Sunderland, those secluded enclaves, the only mainland areas with which she was familiar, were not amongst the chosen sites for the 'meetings held without number', according to the local historian, in villages and hamlets on the coast of Northumberland.)

Conversely Chartists, locked in combat with the shopocracy, would have paid scant attention to the proliferating newspaper accounts of the lighthouse heroine. Thus Grace and the Chartists, both subjects of interminable contemporary news coverage, travelled simultaneously in time, and geographically in close proximity, along parallel lines destined never to meet.

If Grace was oblivious to the high drama being played out in Newcastle and environs, she was equally so to matters that closely touched her and her family's way of life.

The clamorous outcry in town-hall meetings throughout Britain for government regulation of the steamship industry, directly sparked by the *Forfarshire* tragedy and fuelled by Grace's heroic role, drew no comment or word of support from her. One might have supposed that if any public issue could have caught her attention, it would be legislation to protect the lives of seafarers. But even if she had any such notion, it would have been unthinkable for a person of her humble station – and at that, a FEMALE, no matter how INTREPID, HUMANE and NOBLE-MINDED – to speak up about laws and regulations best left to gentlemen such as those who ran Trinity and the Crewe Trustees.

From a class point of view, the Darlings are hard to place precisely. They were not, strictly speaking, 'artisans', 'craft workers' or 'agricultural labourers' although they were highly proficient in the skills implied by these labels. Mr Darling's wages were £70 a year, to which Trinity House would add 'an additional £10 as an annual Gratuity on the production of a certificate of good behaviour from the Agent'. Other perquisites of his employment included cash payment for salvage of cargo from wrecks, premiums for reporting vessels in distress, bounties for saving lives – plus, of course, a rent-free dwelling and an endless supply of fish, game birds and rabbits.

Thus compared to most skilled workers of the period, Mr Darling was extremely well-off financially. But the really distinguishing feature of his job was its total, lifelong security. Untouched by England's economic troubles and the endemic fear of unemployment that beset other workers in town and countryside, Mr Darling in his lighthouse outpost lived in the shelter of the guaranteed patronage of Trinity House, as a rare, highly esteemed protected species, not unlike the birds of today in the National Trust sanctuary on Brownsman.

About three months after the rescue Grace herself was accorded the unique distinction of being placed under the official protection of the Duke of Northumberland. In mid-December 1838, this benign autocrat, supreme ruler of what still amounted to his fiefdom, summoned her and Mr Darling to Alnwick Castle for the purpose of informing them that he had decided to become Grace's legal guardian. In this capacity he would take charge of her growing fund of money. Furthermore, he would advise her on all aspects of her personal life; as reported by Thomasin Darling in *Her True Story*, he told her that 'in cases of troublesome application, matrimonial or otherwise', she should refer the applicants to him.

This development may have been especially consoling because the preceding month had been fraught with horrible aggravations and Grace had been through a very bad time.

By November, the stream of sightseers and journalists had petered out; as daylight hours got ever shorter and storms more frequent the artists, too, had packed up their canvases and gone off to do a bit of creative negotiating with printers and lithographers on the mainland. But the outside world continued to thrust its unwanted attentions on the Maid of the Isles.

For example, the proprietor of the Adelphi Theatre in London wrote offering Grace a clear £50, besides all expenses, for a five-week engagement, with a prospect of another five weeks at the same rate, 'to appear every evening for about a quarter of an hour in a Drama founded upon the preservation of Life in a case of Wreck'. Her only duties would be to sit in a boat while the Drama unfolded on stage. Given Mr Darling's strong disapproval of 'romances, novels and plays', the answer to this proposition would have been easy: a firm and resounding NO. (The drama, entitled *The Wreck at Sea*, was eventually produced at the Adelphi the following February, sans Grace.)

Considerably less clear-cut was a proposal from Mr W. Batty, whose Batty's Circus Royal, featuring 'a Splendid stud of Foreign Horses and Ponies, Wild Zebras, the Royal

Elephant, etc.' plus 'Unequalled Vaulters – Swiss Acrobats – the Infant Actors . . .' was playing to full houses in Edinburgh. Mr Batty gave a benefit performance for the Lighthouse Heroine at which £20 was raised, and he sent his manager to the Longstone to deliver this sum in person together with an invitation to Grace to visit the circus. She replied with a 'sincere acknowledgement for the kindness which you have exhibited towards one personally unknown', adding that 'I will take an opportunity shortly of visiting your arena in person.'

Mr Batty published Grace's letter in the *Mercury*, and followed it up by planting a story in the *Edinburgh Observer*, stating that except for his £20, none of the money reportedly raised for the Darlings had reached them.

From the description, the circus does sound very alluring, and Grace must have been longing to see the Wild Zebras, Royal Elephant, Unequalled Vaulters and the rest. She obviously assumed from Mr Batty's letter that she was invited as a spectator of these interesting events. But some ladies of Edinburgh, self-appointed guardians of Miss Darling's unsullied reputation for modesty and humility, perceived (perhaps correctly) that Grace herself was to be put on display in the arena along with the Swiss Acrobats and the Infant Actors. Accordingly, they wrote an urgent letter cautioning her against 'exhibiting her person in a low circus of Mountebanks . . .'

These insufferable busybodies went on to say,

. . . we would with the utmost sincerity of friendship and admiration of her high character, recommend her *not* to *accept* any such offer; as we are convinced that such a presumptuous step would bring a stain upon those unfading laurels which she has so honourably gained; a *stain*, which could never be effaced. . .

(14 November 1838)

The upshot was that Mr Darling arranged for the *Berwick Advertiser* to print a disclaimer, an 'unqualified contradiction' that Grace had accepted Mr Batty's invitation to visit his arena: 'Miss Darling has no such intention, her present popularity is without her courting and she will take no means of intruding on the public notice' (24 November 1838).

The Darlings' visit to the Duke and Duchess of Northumberland took place on 12 December, a few weeks after these distressing events.

Alnwick Castle, seventeen miles down the coast, is far bigger and grander than Bamburgh Castle. It resembles a walled city, the entrance to which is guarded by a maze of towers and baileys.

'The Barbican or Utter Ward of Alnwick Castle, the seat of His Grace the Duke of Northumberland', engraving by D. Havell after T. M. Richardson, 1 September 1819

Unlike Bamburgh Castle, which long before the Darlings' day had been given over to the charitable enterprises – infirmary, school for poor children, facilities for shipwrecked sailors, etc. – run by the Crewe Trust, Alnwick was (and still is) what social workers call a single-family dwelling, i.e., seat of the Dukes of Northumberland.

The third Duke and his Duchess were prototypically, ineluctably, patrician. He had served as Viceroy of Ireland, she as Princess Victoria's official governess, to which post she was appointed by the Duchess of Kent in 1830 when Victoria was ten years old. (In this capacity she taught no lessons, was merely required to sit in and observe the performance of the Princess's instructors – an arrangement which must have been extremely trying and unnerving for the latter.)

After their wedding in 1818 the Duke and Duchess were accompanied by five hundred of their loyal tenantry, mounted on horseback, for their public entry into Alnwick. Beside the regular Christmas presents to each tenant household of beef and groceries, the Duke made an annual donation of half-a-crown to eight hundred poor men and women who could produce 'testimonials of being of sober and religious habits'. The Duchess sponsored a school in Alnwick village for fifty poor girls belonging to the established Church; daughters of Roman Catholics and Dissenters were specifically excluded.

The Duke, amongst whose official titles were Lord Lieutenant of the County, Vice-Admiral of the Coast, member of the National Institution for the Preservation of Life from Shipwreck, and President of the Royal Humane Society, had dispatched his secretary and other emissaries to Bamburgh immediately after the *Forfarshire* disaster with instructions to get all details of the wreck and rescue. On learning of the Darlings' heroic role, he contributed £30 and the Duchess £10, to the Bamburgh fund for the Darlings and the North Sunderland fishermen. (A year later he was still worrying over the disposition of this fund. On 27 September 1839 he wrote to the Venerable Archdeacon Thorp, one of the trustees, suggesting that the fund should be divided and distributed in three equal parts to Mr Darling, Grace, and the fishermen: 'I well know how jealous that Class of Persons are on the score of strict and impartial justice in money matters and particularly when they trust solely to the honour of their superiors.' He foresaw yet another potential difficulty arising out of the fund, in that '... the whole are in this instance so very much overpaid, that it may produce discontent in future Rescues from Shipwreck'.)

Within a few weeks after the rescue three local branches of the Royal Humane Society had sent Grace silver medals, their highest award for bravery. As president of the national organization, the Duke decided that both Mr Darling and Grace should be given *gold* medals. He embarked on a long correspondence with officials of the society who convened a special session of their General Court – required because hitherto 'a Gold Medallion had never been voted for in any case', as the society's treasurer wrote to His Grace. But he added, 'there is not much to apprehend from setting a precedent as such extraordinary heroism never occur'd before nor is likely to occur again.'

The unprecedented gold medals arrived on the very day of the Darlings' visit to Alnwick. The Duke bestowed the medals, and later wrote to the treasurer of the Royal Humane Society: 'It was truly gratifying to me to witness the very diffident but enthusiastic manner in which these Rewards were received'. The Duchess presented Grace with the letter of 24 November from Queen Victoria, who had sent it to her former governess for safekeeping and transmittal. The Duke announced his intention of making Grace his ward and explained the workings of the trust fund he proposed to establish for her protection. The Darlings were then sent off to the housekeeper, who would give them tea in the servants' quarters, to be followed by a tour of the castle conducted by the castle porter.

The Northumberlands and the Darlings seem to have been made for each other, fitting so neatly into their respective slots ordained by the Creator:

The rich man in his castle
The poor man at his gate
God made them high and lowly,
And order'd their estate ...

At Christmas, the Duke showered the Darlings with all things bright and beautiful. As his letters show he was an inspired chooser of presents, and must have spent much

Portrait of the 3rd Duke of Northumberland by Thomas Phillips

time and thought on what would give the Darling family the most pleasure. He enclosed an itemized list with his Christmas parcel, which included (besides yet more medals and framed vellum notes of thanks from various societies):

For Wm. Darling
A Coat – Jacket – Trousers of waterproof cloth
For Mrs. Darling
A silver teapot to be constantly used by her and afterwards to belong to Grace H. Darling.
Camlet cloak waterproof.
4 lbs of Tea.
For Grace Horsley Darling
A silver-gilt watch with a gold seal and two keys.
Camlet cloak waterproof.
A prayer book with the daily lessons from the Old and New Testaments.
The Prayer book sent by her Guardian may be very convenient to those who are detained at the Light-house on Sundays.
The notes on the Bible are the best that have been published. /signed/ N.
N.B. The two medals, the watch seal and keys are in the inside of Mrs. Darling's teapot.

The garments of waterproof cloth must have been received with joy as the latest thing in lighthouse wear – which they literally were, the waterproofing process having been patented just the year before, in 1837, by Charles Macintosh, FRS, of Glasgow.

With the watch, the Duke sent a letter of detailed instructions:

The watch if constantly worn by Grace Darling will go remarkably well.
To wind up.
Take hold of the ring with the finger and thumb (holding the face of the watch downwards) and press the thumb nail against the spring at the end of the Pillar. The back will then fly open – with the key wind from right to left, that is, looking south; wind from West to East. When the watch is first wound up it is better to wait till the hour is the same as the watch than to attempt to alter the hands . . .

He continued to show solicitude for the welfare of the

Portrait of the Duchess of Northumberland by Sir T. Lawrence watch. In a long letter to Grace of February 1840 concerning the Trust, he adds: 'If your watch should require anything you may send it to me before the 16th of March and I will take it to the maker.'

Judging from the Duke's vast correspondence on the subject, Grace's trust fund became a major preoccupation to which he must have devoted long daylight hours in summer and longer hours of winter darkness. He supervised every detail, from the appointment of the trustees (he chose three high-ranking clerics including the Venerable Dr Thorp, Archdeacon of Durham) to the weighty legal language designed to safeguard Grace's fortune of some £700 for herself, her issue and their descendants in perpetuity.

He wrote to tell Grace that he had sent the trust deed (as elaborate as any for a ducal estate) to a Newcastle barrister, with instructions that the sum of £725 was to be secured in the 3½% public funds, 'interest to be paid regularly to you during your life. Money would be paid in such portions to your children (if you should marry and have any) – or to such of your relatives as you may *by will* appoint.' This clause, unusual in a time when it was customary for the husband to assume full control of his wife's assets, was possibly intended to frustrate designs upon Grace's fund of some future fortune-hunting bridegroom.

Asked if she might want some of the money on hand for spending, Grace replied that £5 every six months would be sufficient. The Duke was delighted by her frugality:

Your Guardian highly approves of you adding to your Capital Fund whatever portion of the interest you can spare; and he is much gratified to learn you continue the same happy, contented good daughter that you were before your prosperity.

Aside from his duties as overseer of Grace's trust fund, the Duke took a keen interest in her marital prospects. He made inquiry of Mr Darling, who replied '. . . that she cannot think of, for every time she goes on shore she gets a catalogue of this one and that other that has made such a bad job of it. But she is going to write herself.'

By the same post (11 November 1840) the Duke had enclosed a letter to Grace:

Longston Light House
Sep.r 3 1839

Mr James Sinclair. Agent to Lloyds (Berwick—
upon Tweed begs to present you with my hand writing

G H. Darling

G H Darling beggs to send her kind reguards
to Mrs & Mr. Sinclair

A sample of Grace Darling's handwriting

Grace Darling,

As I am sending a letter to your father I must enquire how my Ward is going on and whether she is in good health. I see by the newspapers that your brother who jumped first into the boat at North Sunderland, which went off to the wreck of the Forfarshire, is just married: are you likely to follow his example? ...

I hope that the watch continues to go well, if it should want cleaning you may let me have it when I go to Town, and I will take care that it shall be safely returned to you. . .

Her answer:

MY LORD DUKE,

I received yours which you honoured me with, although dated 11th, it did not arrive here until the 24th, and beg to return you thanks for your kind proposal of the cleaning of my watch, but she still continues to go well. . .

I have not got married yet, [and here she had first added] for they say the man is master, and there is much talk about bad masters; [but erasing this she substituted] for I have heard people say there is luck in leisure...

Grace was in the habit of making and keeping drafts of her letters, of which the above is an example reproduced with the changes by Thomasin in *True Story*. Thomasin adds her own reflections:

She had offers of marriage, but none that she entertained. She clung to her father and to her name, and used to say that any husband of hers should take it. She was in the right; it had become a name for sons to be proud of, known throughout the kingdom and beyond.

Grace's determination to keep her own name if she should marry seems to have been her one and only discernible gesture in the direction of what was then known as the Rights of Women, later as Women's Liberation. But, in the event, she never had occasion to put this bold plan into practice.

In April 1842 Grace went ashore for a few weeks to visit her sister Thomasin, who was now a seamstress living in Bamburgh, and various other relations in the vicinity. She caught a chill, and in June wrote to Thomasin that 'I have never been quite free of cold since I was on shore but this last 3 weeks I had been worse. I think it has been influenza but blessed be God I am a good deal better...'

Soon, she was a good deal worse. Reports spread on the mainland about her continuing cough and pallor. She went to stay with Thomasin to be near the Darlings' doctor, Mr Fendler; Thomasin gave up her dressmaking and devoted herself full time to nursing Grace.

Friends and well-wishers, learning of her illness, were full of suggested remedies. As one wrote to Thomasin,

We sincerely wish you could send us better accounts of Grace for whom we feel so much interested. Have you named the asses' milk to her? And does she think she could take a little warm from the ass the first thing in the morning? We have known this of benefit in similar cases and would her medical Attendant approve of her trying Asses' Milk? ...

Grace Darling's last letter enclosed in a letter by her elder sister Thomasin who nursed Grace during her last illness

Another, more concerned with the future of Grace's soul than with such temporal matters as asses' milk, wrote to her:

If you are ill, it is not God's pleasure that your immortal Spirit should derive no benefit from it, on the contrary it is sent with the kindest intentions to wean us from those things which are apt to engross our thought, and to urge and direct us to look forward to a better world beyond the grave. Yes, My Dear Grace, as I said to you before strive continually during your illness to engage your mind on Heavenly subjects...

The Northumberlands did not learn of Grace's illness until September, when they arranged for her and Thomasin to take lodgings in Alnwick village where the Duke's own physician, Dr Barnfather, could attend her. The Duchess called twice, kneeling by Grace's bedside 'to converse the more easily' with the invalid, as Thomasin put it. Eventually Grace and Thomasin moved back to Bamburgh to be among their own people.

Grace wrote a last letter to her parents:

Dear Father and Mother,
    As I cannot write you a long letter this time please God in a little time I will write a long one.
                    I am your loving Daughter,
                    Grace H. Darling.

After that, Thomasin says, 'she went like snow'. A short time before her death she distributed mementoes from her store of presents and medals to members of her family gathered by her bedside. On 20 October she died in her father's arms.

As could be expected, the classes and the masses showed up in profusion at the funeral, held four days later in Bamburgh Church. The *Berwick Advertiser* (29 October 1842) described 'this melancholy event':

At an early hour of the afternoon gentlemen from a distance of many miles round began to arrive, and at the hour appointed, 3 o'clock p.m. the village was crowded with strangers, both rich and poor, many of whom had come a long way to pay their last respects to the memory of the deceased.

Pallbearers listed by the *Advertiser* included the ducal physician, Mr Barnfather; Robert Smeddle of Bamburgh Castle; various clergymen and ten of Grace's relatives.

An immense concourse of people of all grades in society followed, many of whom were observed to be bathed in tears. The scene, altogether, was deeply impressive and affecting.

A bill submitted to Mr Darling on the day of the funeral helps to reconstruct the atmosphere of the occasion. Its elaborately ornate printed heading, in a variety of types, describes the merchandise available:

Bought of George Young
LINEN & WOOLLEN DRAPER
CARPETS, HEARTH RUGS   HATS, UMBRELLAS &C.
FUNERALS FURNISHED
The bill includes:

12 Pair Mens White Kid Gloves	2/4	1	8	0
4 Ladys Ditto	2/2		8	8
8 Pair Mens Blk Kid Ditto	2/4		18	8
5 silk scarfs	12/	3	0	0
3 Bottels of Wine	1/9		5	3

In all, the bill came to £11/16/4, a hefty sum in those days.*

Within a month after Grace Darling's funeral the Venerable Archdeacon Thorp and colleagues set about raising money for her memorial. Queen Victoria sent £20, and Wordsworth contributed his hundred-line poetic tribute, from which a portion was chosen for engraving on a memorial stone in St Cuthbert's Chapel on the Inner Farne Island, about half-way between Bamburgh and Longstone. The choosers may have been hard put to it; they settled for seventeen lines, of which this is a fair sample:

Oh! that winds and waves could speak
Of things which their united power called forth
From the pure depths of her humanity;
A maiden gentle, yet, at duty's call
Firm and unflinching, as the lighthouse reared
On the island rock, her lonely dwelling-place. . .

and so on.

Mr Smeddle, the Darling family and their Bamburgh friends had a better idea: a monument in Bamburgh churchyard overlooking the sea where it could serve as a permanent inspiration to land dweller and seafarer alike. This was built in 1844 by Mr C. Raymond Smith, a London sculptor, after the style of thirteenth-century canopied tombs, its occupant a full-length recumbent Grace complete with oar at her side, fashioned from Portland stone.

*Sent to me by Chris Casson, antiquarian, The Norton Bookshop, Stockton on Tees.

Engraving of Grace Darling's original tomb,
built shortly after her death

Over the next several decades the statue and its surrounding cenotaph kept falling apart, Portland stone proving to be too soft and porous to withstand the buffeting of northern weather. It underwent numerous restorations, notably one in 1885 which came to the attention of one Idawalley Zorada Lewis, lighthouse keeper of Lime Rock, Newport, Rhode Island. She sent a contribution to the fund, duly reported by the Newport *Daily News*, whose special correspondent from Bamburgh described the installation of the new tomb:

After the ceremony, many a kind word was said for Miss Ida Lewis, the 'Grace Darling of America', the light from whose home at the Lime Rock Lighthouse still sends its friendly rays over the waters of Newport Harbor and Narragansett Bay. Many kind wishes are heard on every side here, where she is considered as the sister in heroism of Northumberland's brave girl. If Miss Lewis were able to cross the water she would receive a wonderful ovation among the hardy sons of the Northern coast who hold her name in great reverence. . .

7. AN AMERICAN INTERLUDE

Like a relay runner seizing the baton of her predecessor, Idawalley Zorada Lewis, Heroine of Lime Rock, was born in 1842, the very year of Grace Darling's death. She was the second child and eldest daughter of Captain Hosea Lewis, keeper of Lime Rock lighthouse in Newport Harbor, Rhode Island. In 1858 her father was disabled by a severe stroke; thereafter, she assumed all his duties, which included keeping the boat in good order, tending to the lantern, and, of course, rescuing the shipwrecked. At the age of sixteen, in the year of her father's stroke, she single-handedly saved four young men whom she spotted through her window clinging to their capsized boat offshore. She kept at it over the years and was officially credited with eighteen rescues (some estimates are much higher) by the time of her last one, when she was aged sixty-four.

I first learned of this unusual woman from an article in *Oceans* (November 1985), publication of the Oceanic Society, given to me by a friend when I was hot on the trail of Grace Darling. I corresponded with Frances Harrington, author of the *Oceans* piece, and later with Mr Paul A. Kusinitz of the Newport Historical Society, who sent me quantities of material about the Heroine of Lime Rock.

Even the most ardent Grace Darling booster must concede that IZL's exploits in aggregate far transcended the single Deed of GD, yet today she is virtually unknown in her own country. Nobody of whom I inquired seems to have heard of her – possibly because 'Idawalley Zorada Lewis had an American heart' doesn't trip off the tongue as readily as 'Grace had an English heart'?

According to Andy Warhol, everyone is famous for fifteen minutes. But although she is now largely forgotten, Ida Lewis, as she soon became known to the press, did somewhat better than that in her day. However, while

some of her early rescues were accorded a few lines in the local Newport press, it was not until 1869, ten years after her first, that the *Herald Tribune* of New York and *Harper's Weekly* of Boston picked up the story. Smaller journals around the country followed suit, thus making her a 'household theme, from pine-clad Maine to golden California', to quote George D. Brewerton, her authorized biographer.

In his sixty-six-page booklet *Ida Lewis: The Heroine of Lime Rock*, published in 1869, Brewerton describes in exhaustive detail her first five rescues, prefaced by the

Photograph of Ida Lewis, date unknown

Heroine's own certification that they are 'truly told, the particulars having been furnished.by myself'. She commends the book 'as a faithful record, and the only one I have authorized to be given to the world'.

It is clear from this account that Ida Lewis, like Grace Darling before her, was a paragon of courage, selfless devotion to duty, compassion for her fellow man, etc. But there was a missing ingredient in her rescues: no valuable luxury ship broken on the treacherous rocks with attendant disastrous loss of life to fire the public interest. In fact the unfortunates saved by Ida were for the most part pleasure-seekers out for a sail, whose inexperience with boats, or their own delinquent behaviour, led to their difficulties.

The four boys, 'sons of gentlemen', of her first rescue had got up to some silly pranks which caused their boat to overturn; they prudently refrained from mentioning the matter to their parents, who did not learn of it until after Ida's status of Heroine had already been established in the newspapers. Her second effort, eight years later, involved a party of inebriated soldiers one of whom 'in a drunken frenzy dashed his foot through the bottom of the frail boat' – which, it turned out, belonged to one of Ida's brothers, who had tethered it near the shore. Ida rushed out in the lighthouse craft to lug the soldiers, some sodden and inert from drink, off the sinking boat. Again, her shame-faced beneficiaries preserved a discreet silence about the adventure.

In the third rescue two Irishmen, chasing an escaped sheep that had swum out to sea, had borrowed the same unlucky brother's brand-new skiff and wrecked it. Ida saved the men, and then went back for the sheep which she lassoed and towed to safety. Apparently boat borrowing, or stealing, was a common pastime in those parts, for the fourth rescue was that of a man who had also wrecked somebody else's boat; the owner sent Ida a message to the effect that he would gladly have given her fifty dollars if she had let the fellow drown.

Finally two solid citizens, who had no reason to fear public acknowledgement, came forward to describe the event to the press, declaring that they owed their salvation to Ida's 'dauntless courage and self-sacrifice'. They were soldiers from the nearby garrison at Fort Adams who on 29 March 1869 had hired a sailing boat managed by a young boy. A fierce storm blew up, and the boat capsized. The boy was drowned but the soldiers managed to hang on to the wreckage, and were seen by Ida from the low tower that housed the lighthouse lamp. With the help of her younger brother she rowed out to the drifting wreck and got the men safely back to the lighthouse.

The grateful soldiers having spread the word, the New York *Herald Tribune* sent a reporter out to Lime Rock, and on 15 April 1869 carried its seminal account:

. . . toward the close of a stormy March afternoon, Ida Lewis, the intrepid daughter of the Lime Rock light-keeper, in Newport Harbor, performed a deed that places her side by side, in point of self-sacrificing courage, with the Grace Darling of England, and rounds a career of even greater usefulness in the saving of human life.

Deploring the inadequacy of recognition and suitable rewards for the newly discovered heroine, the writer continued:

In France or England, such a heroine would have long since received many honorable and substantial testimonials, but scarcely any gifts were made to Miss Lewis until two soldiers, rescued on the 29th of March, insisted on her accepting a gold watch and chain of Swiss manufacture, valued at $100. L. Prang, the Boston chromo publisher, sent her last week a kind letter and half a dozen choice pictures. John Carter Brown, esq. of Providence, and John Auchinloss, esq. of New York have each sent her a check for $25; and a Boston gentleman transmitted to her last Friday the sum of $100.

After this appeared, tributes, gifts and letters poured into Lime Rock. The commanding officer of the 5th Regiment US Artillery sent $218 contributed by the officers and men stationed at Fort Adams as a token of appreciation for rescuing their two comrades. The Life Saving Benevolent Association of New York sent a silver medal inscribed to Ida and a cheque for $100. The Secretary of State for Rhode Island forwarded a resolution of commendation passed by the Rhode Island General Assembly.

By the Fourth of July, George D. Brewerton writes, 'the people far and wide, seemed to have "Ida upon the brain". The boys wore "Ida Lewis" hats and ties, and the girls knotted their scarfs Ida-wise, *à la* Rescue.' A fund of

Illustration showing Ida Lewis conducting one of her many rescues

$250 was raised to pay for a magnificent new lifeboat, named the *Rescue*, which was presented to Ida at the Newport Independence Day celebration. Local dignitaries made speeches, among them Mr Brindley, 'the lawyer and classical scholar', who in classical scholarly style compared Ida's life-saving to a famed exploit by Julius Caesar:

If the attempt to secure a roll of papyrus added a brilliant leaf to the chaplet of him whom Shakespeare styles the foremost man in all this world, how transcendent must be *her* greatness who, at repeated times, with fragile arm, has saved, in the aggregate, nearly half a score of men, despairing and struggling in the jaws of the insatiate sea?

The newspapers began referring to Ida as 'America's Grace Darling'; in fact the similarities between the two heroines in looks and temperament are quite striking. Ida, the *Herald Tribune* reports, 'scarcely attains the average height of women, is remarkably slender, and would be thought much nearer twenty than twenty-seven'. She had 'light brown hair, blue eyes keen but kind, cheeks pink flushed though not round enough for beauty, a quick smile, a frank and friendly manner. . .' In another account (Frank Leslie's *Illustrated Newspaper*, 31 July 1869) she is described as 'of a very slight figure, and has never weighed more than 103 pounds [7st 5lb], even when in the best condition, so that her endurance and strength are the more remarkable'.

Like Grace, Ida shrank from the unwelcome consequences of instant celebrity. Brewerton says that from every state in the Union letter writers 'showered their unsought epistles upon poor Ida with a pertinacity in no wise checked by her failure to reply'. She was modest, reticent and conservative, oblivious to public issues that were stirring passions in the world beyond Lime Rock. For example the redoubtable Susan B. Anthony wrote in a suffrage journal applauding her for advancing the cause of women's rights, but Ida did not take kindly to this interpretation of her duties as lighthouse keeper. She told an acquaintance that a visit from Miss Anthony had been a far greater strain on her than rescuing the drowning.

Honours bestowed on Ida, requests made of her, and newspaper accolades closely paralleled those with which Grace had been besieged a generation earlier, albeit with a pronounced American accent. She was the first woman to be given the Congressional Medal of Honor. She was received by President Ulysses Grant and other notable figures of the day, including Admiral Dewey, when they visited Rhode Island. Vaudeville companies in New York begged her (without success) to appear on stage. She inspired at least two musical numbers: the 'Ida Lewis

Mazurka' by E. Mack (the front cover of the sheet music
shows Ida rowing out in what appears to be a rather calm
sea towards a man waving his arm), and the 'RESCUE
POLKA MAZURKA, Respectfully dedicated to the Heroine
of New Port Lime Rock, Miss Ida Lewis' (unsigned) with a
cover drawing of Ida 'in costume as in the rescue of 29
March 1869'.

Of hundreds of letters, many from would-be suitors, one
in particular stands out for its Yankee flavour: an invitation to the 'Complimentary Hop'. One can hardly
visualize anyone having the temerity to invite Grace
Darling to Hop.

And here, a familiar theme: a headline in the Newport
Daily News of 5 August 1869, 'Too much of a Good
Thing', followed by a news story:

Calls begin to come in for locks of hair from the head of Miss Ida
Lewis. We hear that a gentleman from the South wrote to a
friend in the city a few days since, requesting him to procure
such a favor from the lady in question, and that he very wisely
called at a barber shop and obtained a tress of the same color as
hers and sent it to the admirer of the heroine of Lime Rock as the
genuine article. This is a very sensible way of disposing of such
requests.

From his invalid chair, Idawalley's father kept score of the
influx of visitors to the lighthouse, of whom there were
seldom fewer than a hundred per day. The Newport *Daily
News* took note of this (15 August 1869):

The *Tribune* says truthfully that poor Miss Ida Lewis of the
Lime Rock Lighthouse can save her fellow creatures from
drowning, but she cannot save herself from the impertinent
visits of sightseeing jackasses.

Although Ida performed many more rescues over the
years, this intense public adulation seems to have been
relatively short-lived compared to the continuing celebration of Grace Darling's Deed in song, poetry and story.

In the sweepstake of heroinedom, which no less than
that of sainthood seems to have developed over the cen-
turies its own idiosyncratic rules, Grace clearly had some
distinct advantages over Ida. She wasted away from consumption, a disease particularly suited to romantic description, and died young, still a maiden. This circumstance

Respectfully dedicated to the Heroine of New Port Lime Rock.

MISS IDA LEWIS.

IN COSTUME AS IN THE RESCUE OF MARCH 29TH 1869.

Picture by License of Manchester Bros.

J.H.Bufford's Lith. 490 Wash. St Boston.

RESCUE POLKA MAZURKA.   THE OCEAN WAVES DASHED WILDLY HIGH.

✦4✦   ✦4✦

PROVIDENCE, R. I.

Published by CORY BROTHERS, 120 Westminster St.

BOSTON.   PHILADA.
OLIVER DITSON & CO.   JOS. E. WINNER.

To Miss Ida Lewis

Ida Lewis Mazurka

BY

E. MACK.

Philadelphia LEE & WALKER 722 Chestnut St.

A & S. NORDHEIMER Toronto, Ca. Wᵐ H. BONER & Cº 1102 Chestnut St. CHAˢ W. HARRIS N York.

T Sinclairˢ lith

gave rise to much spiritually inspired prose, as in a passage by Mrs Octavius Freire Owen in her book *Heroines of Domestic Life* (Routledge & Sons, *c*. 1860):

Many had sought her hand in marriage, but Grace was enabled to refuse every entreaty to bind the spirit which, for some time past, had been struggling to free itself from alloy, to the fetters of earth. . . As it was, no personal attachment disturbed the frame of peace and resignation in which her fate found her; no sweet earthly dew of tenderness for husband or child left behind, dimmed the pure brilliancy of that hope, that shone like a star through the ruined temple of the soul's frail tenement. So passed she away, calmly and humbly, as she had lived.
'. . . Oh! Happy to have given
Th' unbroken heart's first fragrance unto Heaven.'

As to Grace's youth at the time of her death, Mrs Owen further comments: '. . . she was not perhaps the less blest, that the angel of death wafted away her meek spirit whilst her fame was at its zenith, and time hesitated to wither a leaf of the chaplet gilded, now, by the fadeless tints of Heaven!'

Ida Lewis, on the other hand, lived to a robust old age, succumbing when she was sixty-nine to a prosaic heart attack. She had married a sea captain when in her late twenties – the marriage lasted only two years, after which she returned to Lime Rock to resume her calling as lightkeeper, a post she held for fifty-two years.

Perhaps a bit unfairly, there is no elaborate monument to mark Idawalley Zorada's resting place, no IZL museum with samples of false hair and the 'Ida Lewis' hats worn by boys on the Fourth of July 1869. But as a consolation prize, the local yacht club situated on the Lime Rock bears her name, and is known to this day as the 'Ida Lewis Yacht Club'.

8. THE LEGEND ROLLS ON

Grace Darling artefacts:
Grace Darling pen

Mrs Octavius Freire Owen's perception that Grace's fame was at its zenith when 'the angel of death wafted away her meek spirit' may have been wide of the mark. Judging by the sheer volume of words written about Grace Darling, and artefacts produced bearing her name and likeness, it would seem that her posthumous renown grew with every

Grace Darling Pen

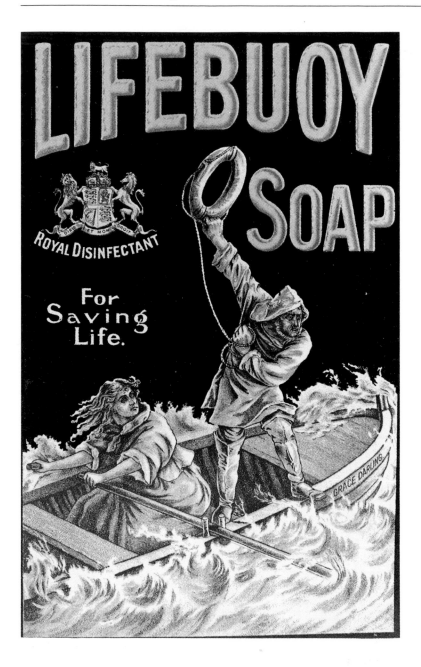

Lifebuoy soap

passing year, to peak towards the end of the nineteenth century, many decades after the angel came wafting.

Two developments on the cultural–commercial front contributed greatly to the consolidation of the Grace Darling legend throughout the Victorian era: the invention of techniques for mass-producing commemorative

OLD TIME-HOME MADE *Grace Darling* CANDIES

SHOPS IN THE LEADING CITIES OF AMERICA STUDIO MINNEAPOLIS

THE FAMOUS *Grace Darling* CANDIES FRESH FROM THE STUDIO

Grace Darling candies

pottery, and the proliferation of girls' magazines and books.

In an age when the use of famous names to advertise products was a new concept in merchandising, Grace Darling's name, like those of Jenny Lind and Fanny Kemble, appeared on a large variety of items – pens, shoes, fireplace implements, hearth tidies, door-stops, napkin rings, soap, chocolates, and all kinds of decorative tableware.

Mugs, plates and jugs bearing the hand-painted likeness of the reigning monarch had appeared as early as Charles II's reign, but these were produced in very limited quantity. In the mid eighteenth century a printer and a potter collaborated in the invention of the transfer-printing process, by which two men could equal the output of a hundred hand decorators. Thenceforth the pottery manufacturers seized every opportunity to immortalize newsworthy people and events on ceramic ware – not only the births, marriages and deaths of members of the Royal Family, but the opening of new bridges and railways, battles on land and at sea, political occurrences from the passage of the Reform Bill to the abolition of slavery – and above all, disasters. Victorians were extremely keen on

Two panels – Longstone Lighthouse and William Darling – from a
four-sided tin tea canister, date unknown

WILLIAM DARLING

these, and the potteries complied with quantities of dramatic pictorial representations of such scenes as a great fire at York Minster, an explosion at Oaks colliery, a ruinous flood in Sheffield.

The *Forfarshire* wreck and rescue, ideal subject for the potter's craft, adorned every conceivable item of ceramic-ware – jugs, mugs, tankards, plates, trays of all shapes and sizes, in a range of materials from lustreware to porcelain to lowly earthenware, priced to suit all purses.

In the twentieth century the vogue for commemorative pottery went into a decline (except for that which continues to celebrate royal events, when the novelty trade springs into action with its Charles and Di plates, its Andy and Fergie mugs), and very little of the Grace Darling pottery survives today. Once in a while one can pick up a piece in a second-hand shop, or at a jumble sale. Emma Tennant paid sixpence some years ago for an excellent mug, on one side of which is the usual picture of Grace straining at the oars, with billowing waves behind her, and on the other side the following poem:

On the Seventh night in September —38
Off Northumberland coast, 'tis sad to relate
Only one half of the ship 'Forfarshire' was there
When from the light-house 'Grace Darling' fair
Espies the wreck amid the surf,
'Twixt the Farne Rock and Northumbrian turf
She with her sire through optic glass discern
Twelve of the crew on the vessel's stern;
But 'Courage, Father,' is the daughter's plea
'A few may be saved. Let us out to sea.'
The maiden rows and courageously saves
Nine of the twelve from their watery graves.

Books and magazines specifically written for girls began to emerge towards the end of the nineteenth century. Children's literature of any kind had been sparse until then; such as there was dwelt mainly on the wicked deeds of children and the just punishment visited upon them by their upright parents. For example in *The Fairchild Family* by Martha Butt Sherwood, published in 1818, Mr Fairchild discovers that his little son has told a lie, so he leads him up to a nearby gibbet and forces him to gaze upon the rotting corpse of a felon as a demonstration of the unpleasant fate that awaits those who stray from the path

Colman's mustard tin, referred to as the 'Heroes' tin – issued between 1906 and 1908. Colman's provide more information: 'The Grace Darling illustration features the only person named on the tin – the other panels illustrate a policeman, lifeboat man, a mine rescuer, and fireman. It held 4lb of mustard and the issuing of the various designs was timed to coincide with the Christmas trade. It is probable that the grocer was able to weigh out small quantities of mustard from these tins which accounts for the size, otherwise they would have only been suitable for hotels and caterers!'

Silver brooch – measuring only 1½ inches – depicting the coble

Representation of the rescue in
Staffordshire pottery

of righteousness. (This episode was omitted from an expurgated edition published in 1902.)

Much of children's lit. *per se* continued to stress the inherent criminality of the young. The children who people the pages of Mrs Edgeworth's *Parent's Assistant* (1796–1800) and her *Moral Tales* (1801) commit most of the Seven Deadlies – Sloth, Envy, Pride, etc. – with predictably awful consequences. The English translation of *Struwwelpeter* came out in 1847 with terrifyingly vivid colour pictures of Harriet in flames, burning to death because she had disobediently played with matches; and Conrad, who sucked his thumb, holding up bleeding stumps after the Long-legged Scissor Man had snipped off the offending thumbs – '"Aha!" said Mamma, "I knew he'd come/To naughty little suck-a-thumb."'

But publications designed for an all-girl readership veered sharply away from the titillating theme of crime and its punishment to a concentration upon Virtue and its rewards. Books about heroines were much in demand, their very titles redolent of piety and moral rectitude. Predictably, Grace, *primus inter pares* (or should it be *prima*?), was prominently featured in all of these, her story told and retold, embellished according to the writer's fancy.

A few titles, with selected fragments from the Grace Darling chapters, may suggest the general tenor:

The Book of Noble Englishwomen: Lives Made Illustrious by Heroism, Goodness, and Great Attainments, ed. by Charles Bruce (1878).
'She was never heard to utter a complaint during her illness, but exhibited the utmost Christian resignation throughout. . .'

Golden Deeds Told Anew by Annie Craig (*c.* 1898).
'Only three years after the wreck of the *Forfarshire* Grace Darling had the summons to go to her Heavenly Home . . . she embarked on her solemn voyage to the unseen world, and was, like Christian, received on the other side by shining ones who welcomed her home.'

Twelve Famous Girls by Marianne Kirlew (undated).
'She helped her mother with the household duties, and grew up quiet, gentle, and reserved. She had the sweetest

nature, and when she smiled it was as if she had caught and kept a sunbeam.' (Marianne Kirlew resurrects the oft-repeated story of the rescued sailor who was moved to tears at the sight of Grace rowing, although the weather-beaten tongue-tied old tar of previous accounts is here transformed into an eloquent chap with a literary turn of phrase: 'Tears filled the eyes of one poor grateful fellow. . . "I thrilled with delight," he said, "when I saw the boat approaching the rock; but the feeling was turned into amazement, which no language can express, when I discovered that two of the oars pulling to our rescue across that awful sea were in the hands of a girl!"').

Girls' periodicals, a spin-off from the newly successful women's magazines, adopted much the same emphasis on virtue as that of the books. The *Girl's Own Paper*, a pioneering weekly whose highly successful format was much copied by subsequent contenders for the growing market for girl readers, stated its editorial objective: 'to foster and develop that which is highest and noblest in the girlhood and womanhood of England'.

To this end, its pages and those of its many imitators were filled with uplifting poems, short fiction and pious sermonettes, interspersed with directions for embroidery, flower-painting and other appropriate maidenly activities. The story of Grace Darling, indubitably a prime example of the highest and noblest, is related over and over again in the mags, and in the year-end bound annuals, recapitulations of their principal offerings.

Yet while Grace was enshrined as what would now be called a role model for the Victorian girl, an occasional note of caution is sounded for those who might misread the message and take things too far – possibly actually try, themselves, to emulate her heroic act. Thus the *Girl's Own Paper* of January 1880 follows a stirring account of Grace's Deed with this caveat to young readers:

As you girls grow older, no doubt in time most of you becoming happy wives and mothers, you will find that the surest way of being useful is, to do first the duty that lies nearest to you; until you have done that, be satisfied not to look further.

The Education Act of 1870, requiring education of both sexes and all classes, seems to have been a matter of continuing alarm amongst writers for the Victorian girl. An article in the *Girl's Own Paper* (*Girl's Own Annual*, Vol. IX, 1887), points to some of the dangers:

. . . the tendency to be impatient of control, to a certain extent brought about by the educational laws, and noticeable in town and country alike, is shown by the fact that those who enter service no longer look up to their mistresses in the way they once did. . .

We say that the education of girls of the masses has a tendency to make them impatient of control; but it must not be supposed that we therefore condemn the education, that is to say so long as it is Christian. . . How is an unchristian education more dangerous than an unchristian ignorance? It is more dangerous, however, because it leads to socialism and revolution.

But every poison has its antidote. Grace Darling's Christian upbringing and selected education as arranged by her father is described in *Everyday Heroes: Stories of Bravery during Queen Victoria's Reign*, published by the Society for Promoting Christian Knowledge. The author concludes that 'It would be well if such a healthy course of reading and instruction could be put before the children of the humbler class today.'

Poetry written extolling Grace and her manifold virtues would fill a large volume. Much of it appeared in the northern press, the work of local Northumbrian writers, adept rhymesters like Miss Elizabeth Younghusband:

And through the sea's tremendous trough
The father and the girl rowed off.

or T. White:

Night, sable goddess reigned with dismal scowl
And Danger's horror seemed aloud to howl.

Fifty years after Wordsworth had eulogized the maiden 'pious and pure, modest and yet so brave', Swinburne took up the theme in his poem 'Grace Darling', printed for private circulation in 1893 and published the following year by Chatto & Windus. Evidently his inspiration for this had been a long-ago visit to William Darling, who had died in 1865, for the last verse runs:

Rowntree's free-gift chocolate tin, c. 1910

Years on years have withered since beside the hearth once
   thine
I, too young to have seen thee, touched thy father's hallowed
   hand:
Thee and him shall all men see for ever, stars that shine
While the sea that spared thee girds and glorifies the land.

   The first verse established the tone:

Take, O star of all our seas, from not an alien hand,
Homage paid of song bowed down before thy glory's face,
Thou the living light of all our lovely stormy strand,
Thou the brave north-country's very glory of glories, Grace.

After many a stanza describing the horrors of the storm
('Dark as death and white as snow the sea-swell scowls
and shines', 'Whence the channelled roar of waters driven
in raging rout, / Pent and pressed and maddened, speaks
their monstrous might and mass') Swinburne returns to
his subject:

Who shall thwart the madness and the gladness of it, laden
Full with heavy fate, and joyous as the birds that whirl?
Nought in heaven or earth, if not one mortal-moulded maiden,
Nought if not the soul that glorifies a northland girl.

Publications intended for the eyes of gently reared young ladies had no monopoly on the thriving legend of Grace Darling. Thanks to the energy of William McGonagall, an itinerant entertainer who earned a precarious living by giving recitations of his poems in the public houses of Glasgow, Dundee and Edinburgh, Grace became something of a folk heroine to the working-class frequenters of those taverns.

In a style possibly better suited to capture the popular fancy than Swinburne's complex prosody, McGonagall produced 'Grace Darling, or the Wreck of the *Forfarshire*' for the pleasure of his public-house audiences. One can visualize half-pints enthusiastically hefted in her praise, and McGonagall's satisfaction in receiving his few shillings' take as the hat was passed.

McGonagall's *oeuvre* is preserved in a slim volume entitled *Poetic Gems*, first published in 1890 when the poet was sixty years old. It has been through many printings since then, the most recent being a handsome boxed edition issued by the Folio Society (London) in 1985.

According to *The Oxford Companion to English Literature*, 5th ed., edited by Margaret Drabble (Oxford University Press, 1985), McGonagall 'now enjoys a reputation as the world's worst poet'. Of the seventeen verses extolling Grace Darling, the following extracts may substantiate his claim to this distinction:

And the screaming of the sea-birds foretold a gathering storm,
And the passengers, poor souls, looked pale and forlorn,
And on every countenance was depicted woe
As the *Forfarshire* steamer was pitched to and fro. . .

Then the terror-stricken crew saw the breakers ahead,
And all thought of being saved from them fled;
And the Farne lights were shining hazily through the gloom
While in the fore-cabin a woman lay with two children in a
    swoon. . .

Around the windlass on the forecastle some dozen poor
    wretches clung,

GRACE DARLING

BALLAD.

Written and Composed by

GEORGE LINLEY.

The heroic Conduct of Grace Horsely Darling, who, with her Father rescued nine Persons from the Wreck of the Forfarshire Steamer, has furnished the subject of this Ballad. The cries of the sufferers were heard by this young female during the night, but the darkness was such as to prevent any assistance being rendered. At Day-break, notwithstanding the storm was still raging, the old Man assisted by his intrepid Daughter, launched a small Boat, each plying an Oar, and after many dangerous and desperate efforts succeeded in safely conveying to the Lighthouse Nine of the surviving Crew.

Nothing but the pure and ardent wish to save the Sufferers from impending destruction could have induced these two humane beings to enter upon so perilous an Expedition, fraught as it was with the imminent hazard of their own lives.

Ent. Sta Hall.

Price 2.6

LONDON,
Published by CRAMER, ADDISON & BEALE.
201, Regent Street & Conduit St.

And with despair and grief their weakly hearts were wrung
As the merciless sea broke o'er them every moment;
But God in His mercy to them Grace Darling sent. . .

Then she cried, 'Oh! father dear, come here and see the wreck,
See, here take the telescope, and you can inspect;
Oh! father, try and save them, and heaven will you bless;'
'But, my darling, no help can reach them in such a storm as
    this' . . .

Then old Darling yielded, and launched the little boat,
And high on the big waves the boat did float;
Then Grace and her father took each an oar in hand,
And to see Grace Darling rowing the picture was grand. . .

Grace Darling was a comely lass, with long, fair floating hair,
With soft blue eyes, and shy, and modest rare;
And her countenance was full of sense and genuine kindliness,
With a noble heart, and ready to help suffering creatures in
    distress. . .

Before she died, scores of suitors in marriage sought her hand;
But no, she'd rather live in Longstone light-house on Farne
    island,
And there she lived and died with her father and mother,
And for her equal in true heroism we cannot find another.

9. GRACE TRANSMOGRIFIED

Of the many full-length biographies of Grace Darling, the first two were published with surprising speed in 1839, less than a year after the Deed: *Grace Darling, or the Heroine of the Farne Islands* by G. M. Reynolds, who later founded *Reynolds's News*, organ of militant trade unionism; and *Grace Darling, or The Maid of the Isles* by Jerrold Vernon, a local writer from Newcastle. Both authors forsook the low road of a mere recapitulation of events surrounding the wreck of the *Forfarshire* for the high road of wildly improbable fiction in which Grace becomes romantically involved with noble personages whose very names ('Somerville' and 'Mordaunt' in Reynolds's book, 'St Clair', 'Fitzroy' and 'Dudley' in Vernon's) suggest their aristocratic connections.

Jerrold Vernon sent Grace a copy of his effort, with an explanatory letter:

... On a perusal of its pages you will find there are various scenes and characters of an imaginary nature introduced, this I trust you will easily excuse as from the miscellaneous nature of your reading you will often have discovered the reins given to Fancy, and that fiction is frequently mingled with the gravest truths for the purpose of adorning a moral and giving point to a tale.

She replied with 'sincere acknowledgments', wishing him 'every success', but added a PS:

Although I have no wish for anything of the kind, permit me to say that a little book wrote after the manner of the *Kent Indiaman*, or the *Rothesay Castle*, would have been much preferred by your
      Much obliged, humble servant,
      G. H. Darling.

GRACE DARLING,

THE MAID OF THE ISLES.

Dedicated to Her Grace

THE DUCHESS OF NORTHUMBERLAND.

" The wheel of fortune turns incessantly round, and who can say within himself,
I shall to-day be uppermost?"—CONFUCIUS.

EMBELLISHED WITH ENGRAVINGS—PORTRAIT OF GRACE DARLING—VIEWS
OF THE WRECK OF THE FORFARSHIRE, &c., BY CARMICHAEL.

Newcastle=upon=Tyne:

PRINTED & PUBLISHED BY W. & T. FORDYCE, DEAN STREET.—TO BE HAD
ALSO OF THE BOOKSELLERS IN LONDON, EDINBURGH, &c.

1839.

This may be as far as Grace ever ventured in expressing criticism, or annoyance; she was not given to speaking her mind on any subject. The Beatles' song about a media star of first magnitude in the firmament of twentieth-century British idols could apply to her: 'Her Majesty is a very nice girl, / But she hasn't got a lot to say.'

In a way, one can hardly blame these writers (each of whom styled his work as a 'novel' rather than a life, or a biography) for spicing up the narrative with a touch of fictional romance. As we have seen, Grace was unremarkable as a personality: pious, obedient, hard-working, modest, there was nothing to distinguish her from countless other English country girls – except for her fortuitous assistance in the *Forfarshire* rescue. This single act of great courage was, in a sense, the sum-total of her.

Thus she became a sort of blank slate upon which the writer could construct his own version of her life, and pursue his own ruminations as to the significance of her story.

Writers in thrall to their publishers, who in turn keep an anxious eye on the shifting tastes of the reading public, tend to fall in line with the literary fashions of their day. Thus four books about Grace Darling, published over a span of more than a century, seem to typify the *Zeitgeist* of their respective epochs:

1875 *Grace Darling, Heroine of the Farne Islands. Her Life and its Lessons*, by the Author of *Our Queen* (Eva Hope).
Era of piety and beautiful sentiments. *GD sanctified.*

1933 *Grace Darling and Her Times* by Constance Smedley.
Era of diligent, meticulous research. *GD's life, her people, her surroundings examined in voluminous detail.*

1965 *Grace Darling: Maid and Myth* by Richard Armstrong.
Era of disenchantment with famous historical personages, and of psychological interpretations of their lives and motives. *GD debunked.*

1984 *Grace; a Play* by Peter Dillon.
Era of eroticism and explicit sex. GRACE DISGRACED!

Grace Darling, Heroine of the Farne Islands by Eva Hope, Walter Scott, Paternoster Square, London.

Eva Hope's book is undated, after the fashion of the day, but evidence points to 1875 as the year of its first publication. I have two editions of this priceless work, procured through a rare-books dealer. Each book has a card pasted on the flyleaf:

Tynemouth Priory Schools *2nd Prize* *Awarded to* *Esther Jones* *for* *Regular Attendance* *J. Fenwick, Head Master*	*Awarded to Claude Jaggs* *for* *English Studies* *Class III* *Henley House, Ware, July 1893*

Claude Jaggs's edition is by far the nicest with a dark red binding, a gold-leaf flower spray on the front, gold-leaf all round the pages and half a dozen plates. Esther Jones didn't fare so well; her edition is fairly drab, navy-blue cloth binding, no decoration, no illustrations – but then she only got the second prize for Regular Attendance.

Next comes Eva Hope's dedication: 'This volume is respectfully dedicated to MISS THOMASIN DARLING, the beloved sister of the heroic Grace Darling, in recognition of her Christian character and amiable disposition, by THE AUTHOR.' (But ungrateful Thomasin, despite this laudatory dedication, soon afterwards published *Her True Story*, which is largely a rebuttal of Eva Hope's extravagant embroidery of the facts.)

In her opening chapter, 'Woman's Work', Eva Hope sets the moral tone, the epigraph a verse beginning:

The rights of woman, what are they?
The right to labour and to pray;
The right to succour in distress;
The right, when others curse, to bless;
The right to lead the soul to God,
Along the path the Saviour trod. . .

'What is woman's work? This is one of the vexed questions of today,' Miss Hope muses. Her answer, after a longish detour into the New Testament, is fairly standard for the period:

She is not, of course, to go abroad seeking work, while work is ready to her hand. She is not to neglect homely duties, for those which call her away from friends and kindred who need her. She is not to stretch out her hands beseechingly for higher service, if they are already full of lowly tasks not yet accomplished. . .

It is surely this which the voice of GRACE DARLING, the heroine whom the hearts of men and women alike agree to love and revere, is saying to us still, and has said ever since her brave deeds thrilled the world.

Before we reach that moment, at page 210, there is much to be absorbed: a chapter on the history of ancient Northumbria; another on the history of lighthouses; one on 'The Childhood of a Heroine'; another on 'The Perils of the Ocean', etc., all heavily interlaced with passages of Biblical wisdom.

Temporal inspiration also has its place, when the highborn Miss Dudley springs out of the pages of Jerrold Vernon's book to make a cameo appearance in Miss Hope's. She, her brother and his friend were rescued by Mr Darling from their foundering yacht, and brought to safety in the lighthouse. 'The guests were evidently persons of gentle birth and habits,' Eva Hope writes. Caroline Dudley and Grace become fast friends: 'The two girls, differently reared as they had been, were yet able to fraternize, and find mutual pleasure in the society of each other.' Miss Dudley was from 'a class of society about which the young lighthouse girl knew nothing. . . Her intellect was of the highest order. . . She had only just left school, which was one of the highest class. . .' She told Grace all about 'the crowded assemblies, the exciting balls, and the endless morning calls'. But she soon returned to her ancestral home, never to reappear in Miss Hope's narrative.

And now, the wreck. Eva Hope sets the scene – storm growing worse 'until even the calm spirit of Mr Darling was perturbed'. Came the dawn, and Grace heard 'piercing, penetrating cries of those whose agony had become almost unbearable'. She sprang out of bed to alert her father, who said that nothing could be done. Much col-

loquy, after which 'Grace's earnest pleading prevailed. . .
"Very well, Grace; I will let you persuade me, though it is
against my better judgement."'

The sufferers on the rock see a boat approaching; and (as
the alert reader will have guessed)

'One is a woman,' said a sailor with moisture in his eyes. 'God
bless her; she is an angel sent from Heaven to succour us.' This
man let the tears stream down his weather-beaten cheeks. . .

All is well, as 'divine strength was behind that of the
slender arms of William Darling's daughter, and the girl's
matchless heroism did not fail her now'.

Fast-forward past the arrival at the Longstone, the
tender care lavished by Grace and her mother upon the
nine survivors . . . past many pages about Grace's fame,
her modesty, poems written about her: 'Grace Darling
never for a moment forgot the modest dignity of conduct
which became her sex and station. . .' Past the visit to the
Northumberlands in Alnwick Castle, in which Grace is
too bashful to speak, and Mr Darling is constrained to say
to the Duchess,

'Your Grace will, I hope, kindly pardon my daughter. She is
overwhelmed by the condescension of your Grace, and that of
the Queen; but, indeed, I know that she is most anxious to
thank you, and does it in her heart, if she cannot trust herself to
put her sentiments into words.'

And it's off with Mr and Miss Darling to the housekeeper's
room 'to partake of some refreshment'.

After this thrilling visit, it's downhill all the way. In
chapter XVI, 'An Early Death', we learn that 'The Duchess
was unwearied in her kindly attentions and immediately
procured good lodgings for Grace in the best and most airy
part of the town.' But 'it was seen that a stronger hand than
those of the human friends around her, was gently leading
her into the "valley of the shadow of death"'.

Finally, Miss Hope's summing-up of Grace:

There is only one report concerning her, and that is, that she was
the personification of pure and simple goodness. It would not
have been very wonderful if the tongues of malice and envy had
found something hard to say of her; but we never hear of the
shadow of a suspicion of any kind having rested upon her fair

name. She possessed in herself the three Graces – Faith, Hope and Charity...

(Alas, Miss Eva Hope! Had you but the occult power to peer into the future, a century hence – more or less – you would hear the tongues of malice a-wagging, you would see descending upon Grace's fair name the deepest shadow of an unmentionable suspicion harboured by two late-twentieth-century writers, Richard Armstrong and Peter Dillon. But I anticipate...)

Grace Darling and Her Times by Constance Smedley, Hurst & Blackett, 1932.

A review in *The Times Literary Supplement* (10 November 1932) betrays a certain restiveness about the sheer length of this book: '... Here is a biography on a scale which would entitle the public man who now has two volumes to have ten... Miss Smedley would have been wise to leave out a good deal which may be interesting but is irrelevant.'

Too true. To give an idea of the immense scope of this enormous book (dedicated, by the way, to 'All Lightkeepers and Lifeboatmen'), with a foreword by Commander Stephen King-Hall: in front are 'Sources and Tributaries', two serried pages of names of those consulted by Miss Smedley ranging from dukes, duchesses and other nobility to the honorary secretaries of the Royal National Lifeboat Institution, to curators of many museums, to managers of shipping companies – all the way down to 'my Husband, together with many other friends and unknown correspondents'.

In the back are five appendixes giving the historical origins of the Crewe Trust, of Trinity House and Lloyd's, of industrial inventions, of lifeboats and shipping laws. In between are forty-two chapters divided into parts 1 to 5...

However, the *TLS* review goes on to say: 'Nevertheless she has on the whole justified a "full-dress" biography. It is a vigorous, picturesque and in the main quick-moving story, written with enthusiasm.' It is also an encyclopaedic compendium of detailed minutiae covering every facet of the heroine's short life, her family, her surroundings. C. Smedley's exhaustive and exhausting book is a veritable archaeological quarry, for those with the fortitude to dig through the layers, of family letters, newspaper cuttings, miscellaneous information of all sorts – an invaluable resource for all latecomers to the subject, including me.

But Constance Smedley's greatest, and most lasting, contribution to the memory of Grace Darling – which by the 1930s seemed in danger of eclipse – was her publication one year later of a children's version of her original opus: *Grace Darling and Her Islands*, Religious Tract Society, 4 Bouverie Street, London EC4, 1933. The jacket copy quotes Lord Baden-Powell: 'A story which should appeal with special force to Girl Guides.' This short volume, a merciful 190 pages of large print, tells almost everything one would want to know about Grace, her upbringing, her Deed, written in a style presumably adopted by Miss Smedley in the hope of capturing the attention of the young reader: 'What a cheerful island! Sheep baa-ing, sea birds calling, land birds singing, and the Darling children and their cousins calling, laughing and singing too.'

The real purpose of the book is revealed at the very end, in a full-page announcement headed 'GRACE DARLING LEAGUE. Founder and Hon. Director: Constance Smedley.' The announcement sets forth Rules and Constitution, stating that the Grace Darling League

shall exist for a period of five years: 8 September, 1933 to 8 September, 1938. Its objects are: 1. To establish Grace Darling in history as our Sea Heroine. 2. To build a Memorial Museum at Grace Darling's birthplace on the ground already provided by Lord Armstrong. 3. To promote interest in our shipping and navigable waterways.

And so it came to pass. Miss Smedley's three stated objectives were all fulfilled within the precise time span she had allotted, so that in 1938, centenary of the Deed, the Grace Darling Memorial Museum was opened by the Duke of Northumberland, dedicated by the Bishop of Newcastle, formally entrusted to the Royal National Lifeboat Institution by Lord Armstrong (owner of Bamburgh Castle, who had contributed the land for the museum) – all to the gratification of some three thousand spectators. Wreaths were placed on the Darling graves, suitable hymns were sung – 'Oft in danger, oft in woe',

GRACE DARLING LEAGUE

Founder and Hon. Director: CONSTANCE SMEDLEY.
Chair of Executive Committee: MAXWELL ARMFIELD.
Hon. Secretary: Miss V. BLAKE, 14 HAMPSTEAD WAY, N.W. 11

RULES AND CONSTITUTION

THAT this Association be called the GRACE DARLING LEAGUE.

That it shall exist for a period of five years: 8th September 1933 to 8th September 1938.

That its objects are:

1. To establish Grace Darling in history as our Sea Heroine.
2. To build a Memorial Museum at Grace Darling's birthplace on the ground already provided by Lord Armstrong.
3. To promote interest in our shipping and navigable waterways.

Some principal features of the constitution of the League:

That it shall admit Founder Members on payment of £1 as subscription for the entire five years; and members who shall pay an annual subscription of 2s. 6d.;

That organizations can become Founder Members and appoint a representative to attend Founders' meeting;

That a General Meeting of Founder and Ordinary members, officers and patrons be held yearly in September to receive the Annual Report;

That at least one Social Function, to which the public be admitted, is arranged yearly;

That as much of the funds of the Association as may not be required for immediate use be placed in Coutts Bank, and sufficient for current liabilities be kept by the Treasurer.

The Hon. Secretary should be communicated with for further particulars.

From *Grace Darling and Her Islands* by Constance Smedley

'Fierce raged the tempest o'er the deep', and 'Abide with me'. Newspapers around the country carried accounts of these stirring events.

But where was Constance Smedley, and what had become of the Grace Darling League? They are nowhere mentioned in the newspaper reports. Seeking answers, I wrote to everyone I could think of who might shed some light on this, including officers of the Royal National Lifeboat Institution both local and national; the Hon. Curator of the Grace Darling Museum; custodians of Northumbrian archives; but none could enlighten me. I even wrote a letter to the newspapers asking for information about the Grace Darling League, hoping to flush out responses from some oldtimers who might have belonged. But although I got some interesting replies to my letter, none of my correspondents had ever heard of the league.

I should have loved to be able to include here some indication of the league's progress – minutes of meetings, amounts of money gathered during the five years of its existence, numbers of members recruited – all the details that make up the day-to-day life of any organization.

As it is, I can only guess that somewhere along the line Miss Smedley may have had a drastic falling out with the other Grace Darling Memorial Committee members. Possibly some PhD candidate, writing a sociological paper on Little-Known Committees, Past and Present – or some such theme – may yet find out the answers to this mystery.

Grace Darling: Maid and Myth by Richard Armstrong, J. M. Dent, 1965.

The epigraph clues us in as to the author's intention:

A good girl about whom a lot of nonsense was talked.
                    Ven. Archdeacon Thorp of Durham

The venerable archdeacon certainly had a point; but would he have endorsed Richard Armstrong's major theses? Not likely.

Armstrong set out to refute the nonsense, and to demythify the Maid. In so doing, he incurred the fury of Commander W. M. Phipps Hornby, Hon. Curator of the

Grace Darling Museum, recorded in headlines in the north of England press:

'CURATOR OF GRACE DARLING MUSEUM REFUTES ALLEGATIONS IN NEW BOOK'
— *Berwick Advertiser*, 10 June 1965.

'BOOK ON NORTH HEROINE STIRS CONTRO-VERSY: GRACE DARLING IMAGE IS KNOCKED BY AUTHOR'
— *Evening Chronicle*, Newcastle-upon-Tyne, 2 June 1965.

The *Evening Chronicle* quotes Commander Phipps Hornby as saying, 'I have made a list of Mr Armstrong's mistakes and they cover six pages of foolscap paper.'

Those six pages, plus a page-by-page refutation of Armstrong in carefully written margin notes, are now in the possession of the present Hon. Curator, Mr Derek Calderwood, who keeps them under lock and key. The Commander Phipps Hornby annotated Armstrong is perhaps the rarest of all rare books, lent to me by Mr Calderwood for a delightful afternoon's read.

Mr Armstrong's book is written in a relentlessly breezy style, with many a (then) up-to-date Hollywoodish turn of phrase: 'the engravers struck it rich. . .' 'periodic windy burps of minor poets. . .' 'Miss Smedley proceeds to destroy Reynolds utterly with a single contemptuous backhanded swipe.' It is embellished with many a quaintly contrived metaphor: 'Her story, full of gaps and throwing up questions like a hotbed sprouting mushrooms. . .'

Commander Phipps Hornby rides forth to do battle like a knight of old — or rows forth like a lighthouse keeper of old — to rescue the reputation of the Heroine, by then dead for 120 years, and the reputation of her father. For example, Armstrong says that Mr Darling 'seems to have been a wild sprig'. P.H. margin note: 'On what evidence does the author conclude that William Darling was a "wild sprig"?'

The Commander is at his most effective in dealing with Armstrong's contention that both Thomasin and Grace were afflicted with hare-lip. On page 52, Armstrong describes Thomasin, eight years older than Grace, as 'dark, waspish and hare-lipped'. Again, on page 70: 'Hare-lipped Thomasin, doomed to be a spinster. . .' and on page 80, 'It is known that Thomasin had a hare-lip. Could it be that Grace was similarly afflicted, and the fact subsequently concealed because it didn't go very well on a national heroine?' Phipps Hornby, expert witness for the defence: 'I disbelieve that. In thirteen years at the museum it is the first time I have heard such a thing. I have examined with a magnifying glass, a photograph taken of Thomasin late in her life and there is no suggestion of a hare-lip. I am certain Grace did not have one.'

Mr Armstrong's evidence of the Heroine's deformity is indeed far-fetched. He cites as proof that all the portraits of her show a small, perfectly formed rosebud-shaped mouth, drawn so as to conceal the cleft. In view of the fact that all girls, from Queen Victoria on down, had rosebud lips in the portraits of the day, this does seem a trifle unfair. But he returns to his unappetizing supposition time and again when discussing the many portraits of Grace: 'The requisite shaping of the mouth is certainly present in all of them in varying degrees, and it could be that in each case the actual cleft was deliberately omitted.' Of John Reay's painting he writes, 'There is no escaping the compressed mouth and the prognathous jaw. That adenoidal expression so marked in people with hare-lip is very strongly suggested.' Another artist, T. Musgrove Joy, 'seems to emphasize the ponderous lower jaw and makes the face appear dished, with the mouth, particularly the lower lip, pushed in'. David Dunbar's marble bust shows 'the small compressed mouth and a strange shrinking or defensive expression. There is also a certain masculinity or at least a vague sexual ambiguity about the head. . . Dunbar also strongly features the massive jaw.'

Furthermore Armstrong strongly hints that Grace Darling may have had an incestuous relationship with her father, although he doesn't quite dare come out and say so. He disputes 'the suggestion of an idealized, almost sanctified relationship between her and her father. One long cool look shows this couldn't have been . . . . she was a woman now, and, in the process of becoming one, her relationship with him had changed. . .'

Poor Grace! Facially disfigured, sexually ambiguous! Poor Mr Darling! In fact, poor everyone in this book who came under the gimlet-eyed scrutiny (as he himself might have phrased it) of R. Armstrong.

All his characters, from the Darlings to the Berwick

bonnet-makers to the North Sunderland fishermen to Mr Smeddle of the Crewe Trustees, are motivated by greed, status-seeking, a desire to cash in on the shipwreck and on Grace's subsequent fame. Mr Darling and the fishermen rushed out to the wreck in an unseemly race for the cash bounty payable to rescuers. When the fishermen discovered that Mr Darling had got there first, 'they were injured in their most sensitive part – the pocket – and being the sort of men they were they must have told him so with variations and full orchestration. It is a safe guess that there was a fierce quarrel in the Longstone that morning. . .' Likewise, wily, self-seeking Mr Smeddle, in a series of behind-the-scenes manoeuvres involving the Duke of Northumberland, the press and the Royal Humane Society, sought to enhance his own prestige via his devious exploitation of Grace.

As to the famous beaver bonnet, presented by the hatters of Berwick-on-Tweed, Mr Armstrong says that 'There is no proof of course that the gift was anything else than genuine and spontaneous. But it would be interesting to know how many of their hats were sold . . . more interesting still to know if Mr Smeddle was involved in the scheme, and what sort of a rake-off the Darlings got, if any. On these points the records are silent.' An acerbic margin note by Commander Phipps Hornby: 'Possibly because there was nothing to say', which is rather a good point.

According to Armstrong, Grace Darling died not of consumption as is generally believed, but of a psychosomatic illness brought on by the unwelcome public acclaim, her persecution by the press and the trustees of the Grace Darling fund, who 'played their part in harrying her', the incessant letter-writing forced on her by myriad fans – all orchestrated and manipulated by the villainous Mr Smeddle.

The *coup de grâce*, says Armstrong, was delivered by the Duchess of Northumberland when she arrived unannounced at Grace's bedside: 'The very sight of the elegant great lady must have disturbed Grace profoundly. . . It could be that the visit of the duchess itself was the turning point. . .' Soon after, Grace 'turned her face to the wall' and died.

While *The Times Literary Supplement* may not have had the benefit of Commander Phipps Hornby's astringent comments, their reviewer reached some of the same conclusions. '[The author's] own fancy twines and burgeons as luxuriantly as convolvulus,' he writes. He scoffs at Armstrong's notion that Grace was driven to death by the pestering of admirers: '... the author becomes airborne... There is certainly evidence that she was fussed when the business got out of hand... That hardly adds up to sickness unto death.'

Grace, a play by Peter Dillon, Iron Press, 5 Marden Terrace, Cullercoats, North Shields, Tyne & Wear, 1984.

If Richard Armstrong's account seems to have reached rock-bottom as a downbeat reconstruction of the characters in Grace Darling's world, there is worse to come. The reader who found Armstrong's book unsavoury will find Peter Dillon's play positively revolting – enough to make your hair curl. Yet in spite of – or perhaps because of? – its subversive implications, the play was surprisingly well received by theatre critics in the conservative north: 'Passionate and compelling; the audience was spellbound' – *Alnwick Advertiser*. 'Skilfully performed' – *Scotsman*. 'A well-researched and important piece of regional theatre' – *Northern Echo*.

Peter Dillon's play was written, according to the jacket copy, 'as part of his Arts Council funded year as writer in residence with Northumberland Theatre Co. in 1982... Dillon's work points an accusing finger at many parties, including nobility, who used Grace Darling to their own ends.'

That it does. There are no heroes in the play, only villains – and no heroine. In a letter to me, Peter Dillon credits Richard Armstrong's book as his primary source, suggesting a 'triangular relationship between Grace, her father and Smeddle... The machinations of Smeddle, the Duke and Duchess of Northumberland, and the newspapers of the day set me on to seeing Grace as a victim rather than a heroine ... a story that begins with the wrecking of a steamboat and ends with the wrecking and crushing of a human being.' Grace is indeed wrecked and crushed in Peter Dillon's play, and so is everyone else in the drama.

Grace comes through as a snippy, tiresome young thing,

self-centred and sly, always on the make. Mr Darling is interested in only one thing: money. The Duke and Duchess of Northumberland have become absolute monsters – reincarnations of Lord and Lady Macbeth. In fact at one point the Duke exclaims, 'Out, out, damned spot!' although from the stage directions we learn that he is actually only trying to remove a blackhead from his chin.

Incest, inferred and covert in Richard Armstrong's book, is here explicit and overt:

DARLING: You're the best to me, lass.
[*They cuddle unfatherly/daughterly.*]
GRACE: I love you, Father.
DARLING: And I love you.

At Alnwick Castle, the incestuous pair are caught *in flagrante*:

GRACE: Just hold me.
DARLING: I daren't not, in here. Howay then, quick. [*Grace and Darling embrace. The Duchess and Smeddle enter.*]
DUCHESS: O, my goodness, how very touching.

The real motive of the Northumberlands in adopting Grace as their ward is now unmasked.

DUCHESS: The Darlings are Northumbrians, think of what we stand to gain.
DUKE: They are my people. Loyal subjects, no doubt.
DUCHESS: Then do your duty, in other words, rather you tell the story than somebody else does. We're going to win first prize.
DUKE: What is that?
DUCHESS: Grace Darling, of course.

When Grace is dying, the Duchess comes prying in her intrusive way. She asks if there is anything she can do, to which Grace answers 'Go away and leave me be.' Enter Mr Darling – same old theme, 'Hold me, Father. Quickly, hold me.' As they embrace, Grace natters on in her wheedling, grasping fashion about a silk gown once promised by faithless Mr Smeddle. She dies.

CURTAIN
(And none too soon, for this reader.)

10. ENVOI

In the course of writing this book I discovered that Grace Darling is constantly being re-invented according to the bent of those with whom I discussed her.

An American friend, distressed by the lack of any romantic interest in Grace's story, suggested that she may have actually lured the sailors to their doom by sun-bathing naked on the Big Harcar rock. It's a sweet thought, I said, but not terribly likely, as anyone can attest to who has sampled the mean temperature in those parts (and 'mean' is the *mot juste*), or who has seen those jagged, unwelcoming rocks.

Opinions of English women in their mid-thirties or their forties, who still recollect versions of Grace from childhood reading, vary sharply.

Marina Warner remembers her as a character in a weekly comic magazine called *Girl*, to which she subscribed when a small child. As *Girl* is not readily available in libraries, I asked Marina to recall what she could about Grace Darling. 'There were picture strips of her alone in a little rowboat, dashing out to the rescue. And she died in the attempt, not only a heroine but a martyr.' Not quite accurate; but Marina, author of *Joan of Arc: The Image of Female Heroism* and a foremost authority on heroines and martyrs, may be inclined to confer such attributes with a lavish hand on those who caught her fancy when she was four or five years old.

Most surprising, to me, is the reaction of the advance guard of the feminist movement, militant young women bent on consciousness-raising and the like.

Two of these wrote to give me their views of Grace Darling. The first, in her early thirties, said 'She was a soft, stupid girl who was the very reason I had to run around in skirts and was not allowed to run around in trousers and Wellington boots.'

The second, in her early forties, was equally vituperative. 'I hate her,' she wrote. 'Not her, but the packaged version that was slipped into my breakfast cereal as a girl. When I think of her wild eyes and arms pounding I know of course that she was *really* fleeing the Victorian mythmakers. Even in that distracting storm she had picked up the scent of what was to come, and the generations of young women who would have their hopes and aspirations neatly trimmed by the Appropriate Female Heroine, themselves set out on butterfly pins.'

Why does the shade of Grace Darling, dead for almost a hundred years before my correspondents were born, arouse such venomous loathing?

Clearly, she was neither 'soft' nor 'stupid', and can hardly be held responsible for a dress code enforced on a girl who grew up in the 1960s.

And was Grace really fleeing the Victorian mythmakers, or was she simply trying to rescue the shipwrecked?

ACKNOWLEDGEMENTS

Most of the books I consulted, and the people who helped – to all of whom I am most grateful – are acknowledged in the text. I am also indebted to many others:

Early on, I had the good fortune to secure the services of Christian Milner as researcher. Quick-witted, fleet of foot and possessed of a keen sense of humour, he got the point of the book in a flash and nipped about from hither to yon fetching material from the British Museum, the Colindale newspaper library, the Bodleian. He supplied extensive notes on a variety of subjects, ranging from early steam-ships to nineteenth-century journalism to the social history of the period, on which I have drawn liberally.

Amongst the books he recommended was *Women's Magazines, 1693–1968* by Cynthia L. White (Michael Joseph, 1970), a fascinating source of information on girls' magazines. He also put me in touch with Tessa Chester, curator of the Renier Collection in the Bethnal Green Museum of Childhood. My thanks to her for sending me photocopies of many articles about Grace Darling in girls' publications.

A pleasurable aspect of writing is the way friends often swing into the act, producing unexpected nuggets of use-ful information. I first noticed this when writing *The American Way of Death*; even chance acquaintances encountered at parties were avid to tell about their mother's awful funeral, or how they outwitted an under-taker when putting away dear old Dad. My experience with this book was a bit different. When asked 'What are you writing these days?', my answer, 'a book about Grace Darling', was often a conversation-stopper in California where I live, as nobody there had ever heard of her.

There were, however, exceptions, most notably Jerome Garchik, a lawyer, and his wife Leah, columnist at the San Francisco *Chronicle*. Luckily for me they somehow got hooked on the subject and plied me with all sorts of invaluable books and articles. Amongst their offerings: *Commemorative Pottery, 1780–1900* by John and Jennifer May (Scribner, 1973) and *Murder and Moralities: English Catchpenny Prints, 1800–1860* by Thomas Gretton (British Museum Publications, 1980). I extracted much information from these charming volumes. Above all, the Garchiks – like many Californians ecology-minded nature-lovers, members of such esoteric groups as the Oceanic Society – sent me a copy of *Oceans*, without which I should never have known of the existence of Idawalley Zorada Lewis.

There were other 'angelic encouragers', as the late Philip Toynbee described people who took an interest in his work-in-progress. Nora Sayre wrote to me from the Thurber House in Columbus, Ohio, where she was spending some weeks as writer-in-residence, about a passage she found in *The Thurber Album*: 'He mentions "the muddy colour print that depicted the brave and sturdy Grace Darling pulling away from a yellow lighthouse on her famous errand of mercy".' The picture belonged to Thurber's childhood nurse, born about 1830 in the Middle West. So – Nora suggested – 'perhaps the picture of Grace on her wall is an indication that the legend of Grace Darling *did* cross the ocean?'

A further indication was noted by Nancy E. Lee, head of the Special Collections and University Archives in the California Polytechnic State University, San Luis Obispo. She tells me that an early American filmstar assumed the name Grace Darling as her *nom de théâtre* and acted in a 1916 silent serial entitled *Beatrice Fairfax*.

My letter-to-editor asking readers for any information they might have about the Grace Darling League produced some surprising results. It was sent to all the major London newspapers and weeklies, which generated a tiny handful of replies – two of which were, however, of much interest: Miss Margaret Gardiner, a longtime friend of mine now in her eighties, saw my letter in *The Times Literary Supplement*. She sent a vivid word-picture of Constance Smedley, whom she had known as a child: 'I disliked Constance. She was dogmatic, bossy, ruthlessly righteous and alarmingly energetic.' I enjoyed that description, as it confirmed my preconceptions of GD's prolific biographer. (Could these characteristics have been

the reason that Miss Smedley was excluded from participation in the GD museum opening? I wondered.) And
Peter Dillon, who read my appeal in *The Times Educational Supplement*, sent me his amazing *GRACE*, just
what was needed for Chapter 9.

That was about the size of it from the national press, but
when the same letter was published in several northern
dailies from Yorkshire to Scotland, the response was
tremendous – replies poured in, attesting, I suppose, to the
highly regional factor in perpetuation of the GD legend. In
the north, Grace is alive and well. I am grateful to all those
who took the trouble to write. Two in particular sent
valuable information:

Chris Casson of the Norton Bookshop, Stockton on
Tees, saw my letter in the Newcastle *Evening Chronicle*.
He has a large collection of Darling memorabilia including many letters from Grace's brothers and sisters, and the
original bill to Mr Darling for Grace's funeral furnishings.

Mrs H. Chitty of Conbridge, Northumberland, read my
letter in the *Hexham Courant*. There ensued a delightful
correspondence, in the course of which Mrs Chitty introduced me to the work of M. A. Richardson, author of *Local
Historian's Table Book* – as she said in her letter, 'as full of
good stuff as new-laid eggs'.

My sister Deborah Devonshire, who like Mr Darling is a
keen gardener, spotted the Grace Darling rose in the
current Peter Beales rose catalogue. She found the
advertisement with colour photo of Royal Doulton's
statuette of Grace. She also sent me a photocopy of the GD
entry in the *Dictionary of National Biography*, in which
Eva Hope's book is listed as 'one of two unsatisfactory
biographies'.

Unsatisfactory to the *DNB*, perhaps, but not to me.
James MacGibbon, formerly of Curtis Brown and my first
literary agent, tracked down two copies of this invaluable
book at my husband's request for a surprise birthday
present.

Madeau Stewart of Burford, a Grace Darling *aficionada*
from childhood, gave me her cherished copy of Constance
Smedley's book, and permission to photograph her picture
of the rescue bought in a Burford antique shop.

Robin Gard, MA, county archivist for Northumberland,
has custody of the Darling family papers, including Queen

Victoria's letter to Grace of November 1838. He sent me
stacks of material, among which was some correspondence between Constance Smedley and an
unfortunate Mr Oxberry, a museum custodian. Smedley
to Oxberry, 19 April 1932: 'The book cannot delay much
longer. I ought to have that bundle, and I really need it all,
by next Monday.' Dogmatic and bossy, as Margaret
Gardiner had noted; but Mr Oxberry dug in his heels. His
reply of 22 April 1932: 'I am extremely sorry to say so but
there is no possibility of my finding time to spend the
many hours that will be required to go through the unas-
sorted mass of notes. . .' Good for Mr Oxberry, says I.

Mr Gard was immensely helpful. He got in touch with
counterparts and librarians throughout the north, who
produced such items as the pro-and-con Chartist posters
and a leaflet from the Green Cross Society: 'NOVEMBER
24th IS THE BIRTHDAY OF GRACE DARLING. . . On
Saturday, 24th November, 1934, let us unite in planting a
complete national Memorial of GRACE DARLING
TREES.' The leaflet explains how to go about forming a
provisional committee, securing a charter, finding a suitable site, etc. (How many trees were planted? Have they
survived? Over to other researchers for the answers.)

My assistant Catherine Edwards, besides performing
myriad tasks to alleviate the normal strains of everyday
life, did a brilliant job of organizing and keeping track of
the overflowing Grace Darling files which filled two huge
boxes. There were times when the house looked like a vast
Lost and Found depot – quantities of letters, books,
pamphlets, old newspapers Lost by me and Found in a
trice by Katie Edwards. She and Mary Jane Makar, two of
the speediest and most efficient people I have ever met,
shared the work of typing the final draft of the manuscript.

When two or three writers are gathered together, the
conversation is apt to turn to a bitter denunciation of their
publishers, with complaints ranging from lack of editorial
attention to failure to answer letters.

Happily for me, none of the above applies to my experience with the publishers of this book, whose cooperation
at all stages was exemplary.

Tony Lacey of Penguin picked up on the idea from Bob
Treuhaft's chance suggestion, and encouraged me to submit a proposal. Soon after that, Bob and I had a meeting
with Tony and Susan Rose-Smith, then Penguin's picture

researcher. To my amazement, although GD was at this stage a mere twinkle in the eye consisting of a three-page memo, Susan had already mined the BBC archives and lots more, and had turned up marvellous Grace Darling graphics (as we call them in the publishing trade). She kept at it, constantly finding more pictures, and enlisted the services of Eddie Ryle-Hodges, expert professional photographer, to dart around Bamburgh and environs with his trusty Brownie – or whatever cameras are called these days – to assemble the lovely pictures that adorn this book. Tony Lacey's able assistant Tessa Strickland was a super-prompt correspondent, steering things through the uncertain shoals of manuscript-to-galleys. My agent Deborah Rogers gave invaluable advice at all stages of this rather aberrant (for me) endeavour.

My gratitude to William Abrahams of Dutton, the American publisher, is unbounded. He is almost a neighbour – at least in Calif. terms – living about an hour's drive (on one of those often lethal freeways) from our house. He never failed to respond to my constant *cris de coeur*, would come dashing over with his longed-for editorial advice, and with his swift pencil would point out where I had gone wrong – here a redundancy, there a hopeless mess of organization, not to speak of misspellings and grammatical mistakes. He went over the whole thing – not once, not twice, not even thrice, but as many times as it took to get it in acceptable shape.

So it was a three-way publishing venture: William Abrahams, responsible for editing the text; Susan Rose-Smith, picture researcher; and Tony Lacey, who pulled the whole thing together into an actual book. Thinking it all over, compared with the contribution of those flowering brains my own seems minimal.

Acknowledgements

Black and white photographs
Courtesy the author, 140, 141, 143 (below); BBC Hulton Picture Library, 124; John Johnson Collection, Bodleian Library, 63, 66; J. Allan Cash, 82, 85, 86; Mary Evans Picture Library, 54, 55; Ferens Art Gallery, Hull City Museums and Art Galleries, 38–9; Alan Greeley (courtesy Madeau Stewart), 28; courtesy Lionel Lambourne, 32–3; National Maritime Museum, 58; National Portrait Gallery, 93; Newport Historical Society, 128, 131, 134, 135; courtesy the Duke of Northumberland, 115, 116; courtesy Robert Opie, 137, 138, 139, 143 (above), 148; courtesy HM The Queen, 26; Eddie Ryle-Hodges, 22, 31, 35, 41, 45, 68, 74, 76, 77, 78, 79, 80, 92, 96, 119, 121, 150, 154; City Museum and Art Gallery, Stoke-on-Trent, 144; by permission of the Chief Archivist, Tyne and Wear Archives Service, 105, 106; Victoria and Albert Museum, 30, 72–3, 112.

The map on page 50 was drawn by Reg Piggott.